JAMES RUNCIE is an award-win̶
and literary curator. He is the author of twelve novels that
have been translated into twelve languages, including the
seven books in the Grantchester Mysteries series. He has
been Artistic Director of the Bath Literature Festival, Head
of Literature and Spoken Word at the Southbank Centre,
London, and Commissioning Editor for Arts on BBC
Radio 4. He is a Fellow of the Royal Society of Literature.
He lives in Scotland and London.

TELL ME GOOD THINGS

On Love, Death and Marriage

James Runcie

BLOOMSBURY PUBLISHING

LONDON · OXFORD · NEW YORK · NEW DELHI · SYDNEY

BLOOMSBURY PUBLISHING
Bloomsbury Publishing Plc
50 Bedford Square, London, WC1B 3DP, UK
29 Earlsfort Terrace, Dublin 2, Ireland

BLOOMSBURY, BLOOMSBURY PUBLISHING and the Diana logo
are trademarks of Bloomsbury Publishing Plc

First published in Great Britain 2022
This edition published 2024

A catalogue record for this book is available from the British Library

ISBN: HB: 978-1-5266-5544-8; PB: 978-1-5266-6777-9;
EBOOK: 978-1-5266-5543-1; EPDF: 978-1-5266-5542-4

2 4 6 8 10 9 7 5 3 1

Typeset by Newgen KnowledgeWorks Pvt. Ltd., Chennai, India
Printed and bound in Great Britain by CPI Group (UK) Ltd, Croydon CR0 4YY

MIX
Paper | Supporting
responsible forestry
FSC® C171272

To find out more about our authors and books visit www.bloomsbury.com
and sign up for our newsletters

For Rosie and Charlotte

Everyone in the world has to face the loss of someone they love. There are countless tributes, biographies and laments written by the recently bereaved. In the best of them, the writing reaches out beyond therapy and recollection to share what Dr Johnson called 'moral instruction in the art of bearing calamities'. They help those facing a similar devastation.

My wife, Marilyn Imrie, died of motor neurone disease at five o'clock in the morning on 21 August 2020. She was a drama director, a singer and an artist: mother to two girls, wife, sister, aunt and grandmother. She was seventy-two years old.

We had thirty-five years together. This is our story, and this book is a love letter to her. But, as well as an account of trauma, it's the memoir of a woman who was an effervescent force for good in the world, a person who thought the best of people, embraced adventure and delighted in greeting her friends: 'Hello, Gorgeousness! Tell me good things!'

This is not only my way of reclaiming her from the last months of a terminal illness but an attempt to provide my own version of Johnson's 'moral instruction' and to offer both the consolation of sorrow and the possibility of hope in the face of despair.

So here you have it. Bereavement: a comedy.

The End

In November 2014, we were staying at Gladstone's Library in Flintshire, some eight miles west of Chester. I had given a talk the previous evening, and Marilyn and I had booked in for a few days to read, think and write in Britain's finest residential library, founded by the Victorian scholar, polymath and prime minister, William Ewart Gladstone. The plan was for a restorative retreat but, on our first morning, Marilyn woke up with a sharp pain down her left arm.

I was making tea. I came back to the bed and touched her wrist, very gently, to ask where it hurt, and she called out in anguish. She gave such a sharp cry that I couldn't quite believe the sound was coming from her. What was this severe and frightening discomfort that had come on overnight?

Marilyn wondered if it was the result of a recent flu jab, even though she had never had such a reaction before. The pain went up to her shoulder and down her left leg. She didn't feel at all well.

We had booked in for the week but decided, during breakfast, that staying on was going to be no good. It would be better to get back home to Edinburgh. Marilyn saw a doctor as soon as we returned and, although the soreness eased, she was thrown by the peculiarity of the inflammation and the inexplicable speed of its arrival.

Over the next few years there were what doctors explained away as 'the aches and pains of ageing': tiredness, moments of numbness, a weakening in the wrists and arms. Marilyn found it hard to twist the tops off jam jars, and we developed a routine where she stopped bothering and handed them straight to me. She complained that the saucepans had become unwieldy, and I was told off for buying a griddle because it was too heavy. 'How do you expect me to lift that?' she asked.

Soon, there were other health issues: oedema in the right ankle, a watery eye, and a pain in her upper leg which reminded us of the joke I had made at my sister's wedding: 'Our mother has just had a hip replacement operation. We did wonder whether it might have been simpler to keep the hip and replace the rest of her.'

These were still days in which illness came and went and we always got better; when we could laugh as if nothing could ever go wrong, or, if it did, we would find a solution and get on with our lives. Marilyn continued to work as she had always done, producing and directing *Rumpole* and *The Ferryhill Philosophers* for Radio 4, the voice-overs for an animation series, a stage musical about Dusty Springfield, and an adaptation of Alice Munro's *The View from Castle Rock* at the Edinburgh Book Festival. We worked on three of my plays together, two about Dr Johnson and one about an imaginary meeting in Paris between Fred Astaire, Audrey Hepburn and Jean-Paul Sartre. We described it as the world's first and probably last musical about existentialism: *Tap Dancing with Jean-Paul Sartre*.

Marilyn had always had amazing energy but started to tire. 'It's not surprising,' I said, 'you never stop.' The children asked if she had thought about taking it more easily, but no one dared suggest the word 'retirement' and in 2017 we celebrated her seventieth birthday in Venice. We bought a house, right by the sea, in the fishing village of St Monans in the East Neuk of Fife, not far from where Marilyn was born. Our daughter, Charlotte, was working as a journalist and writer of non-fiction, and she had just given birth to a baby girl. My stepdaughter Rosie worked in the theatre as a dramaturg. At the time, we did not realise that things could not possibly be this good. We were too busy.

Then came the fall. A slip on a wet stone during the interval of a concert in August 2019. ('My foot just gave way.') Then another on her birthday in November. ('I must have tripped on the leg of a sofa.') Then she fell in the garden but didn't tell me about it until there was another in the living room as she turned away from the window. The doctors asked if she had been drinking. She laughed and looked at me. 'No,' I explained. 'I'm the one who drinks. Marilyn hardly touches the stuff.'

They told us it was probably sciatica. She had physiotherapy but her legs and hips did not seem able to respond as they should have done.

A few weeks later, teaching a course in radio drama at LAMDA, she found that she could not get her mouth to say the word 'vintage'. Alarmingly, she complained that there was something wrong with the accelerator on the car. 'It won't go down.' She lost more strength in her legs. Every time there was a new symptom, she went to the GP. He referred her to what he called a 'one-stop shop', which turned out to be a polyclinic for geriatric patients. They thought she was just getting old. There were no further appointments available for three months.

At Christmas, Marilyn could not lift the turkey in and out of the oven and asked Rosie to accompany her to the shops because she didn't want to go out alone. She was frightened of another fall.

She felt tired and heavy and took more and more painkillers. She never told us how many she was taking. They were hidden by her side of the bed, in the bathroom, in her handbag and in make-up pouches. We were aware something was wrong, but no one knew what, and we started to worry about the big things: a brain tumour, MS, and something called myasthenia gravis, except her watery eye did not seem to be consistent with the disease.

Eventually, we saw the doctor at the one-stop shop. He tested Marilyn's reflexes and asked about her voice and her swallow. At the time, she did not have any problems eating or chewing and he was puzzled by a variety of symptoms that 'didn't add up'.

I could see that the weakness in her voice terrified her. Marilyn was a singer. I had always thought she had the most beautiful voice in the world. Now, it was quiet and hesitant, and I could tell that she was frightened.

'Don't worry,' the doctor told us. 'It's not going to get any worse.'

But it did. The gap between appointments narrowed so that in January and early February we were going for tests twice a week. They said there was a neurologist we should see: a Dr D. But he wasn't available. There was a long waiting list. It was going to be five more months.

Separately, and without telling each other, we looked up the symptoms on the internet. We tried to find out if we could see Dr D privately but, even then, it was going to be a ten-week wait. It seemed that he was just about the only neurologist in Scotland but that couldn't be right. I spoke to my friend Ali, a private doctor in London, who told me to come down south as soon as we could. We needed clarity. She would get a diagnosis immediately. 'Just throw money at it, James. What matters more than this?'

But Marilyn was tired and in pain and could not face the journey. Surely, we could get all this done in Scotland?

We went to the one-stop clinic again. They had lost the last blood test, so Marilyn was asked to give blood by a nurse who told her, 'I hate doing this and I'm not very good at it.' Blood poured everywhere. Marilyn tried to be patient but muttered to me afterwards, 'For God's sake.'

We googled myasthenia gravis and brain tumours and avoided talking about the one illness that we feared the most. Her voice faltered, some food became difficult to chew (although Marilyn disguised this because she didn't want to alarm us, even though we all knew). She asked Charlotte to cut up her green beans for her at one Sunday lunch because she said she couldn't face big mouthfuls.

The doctor asked about her swallow once more, and we pushed for more tests, and he mentioned Dr D again and said that there were more things to investigate because none of this made sense, until he finally ended a sentence with the words that no one had ever dared to say out loud. His voice was gentle and even, but to me it sounded as if he spoke entirely in capital letters. MOTOR NEURONE DISEASE.

I know now, because doctors have told me, that these are the three words they most dread having to say to a patient. They only do so when they have ruled out absolutely everything else. It is the 'last man standing' in a diagnosis, the one disease that you really, *really* don't want to get. MND is the degeneration and death of the specialised nerve cells in the brain and spinal cord (motor neurones) which transmit the electrical signals to muscles for the generation of movement. It is a form of slow and inexorable paralysis. There is no treatment for it; only the delaying tactic of the drug Riluzole, which does not work on everyone. And even then, it only prolongs life by, on average, three months.

Apart from that, there is absolutely nothing to be done. The paralysis takes hold until you are no longer able to speak, move, eat, drink, or, eventually, breathe. With incapacity comes humiliation. MND is not so much insidious as relentless. It is ravenous and without pity. Thickening saliva makes the patient prone to choking. Incapacity causes painful constipation. You never know quite what is going to happen next but there will always be something awful. You can't 'fight' it or 'battle' it. You can't be 'determined to beat this', or any of the other clichés that people say in the wake of a cancer diagnosis. MND is fatal in every single case. And it is not even rare. In the United Kingdom, 1 in 50,000 people get it every year. The individual lifetime risk is 1 in 300 and, according to a recent study, this is increasing. No one seems to know why, despite the millions of pounds and dollars spent on research.

The doctor tried to reassure us that he didn't think it *was* necessarily MND because Marilyn still had her swallow, and so we tried hoping that it was myasthenia gravis or even a brain tumour. 'Imagine hoping for a brain tumour,' she said. We were told that the nearest-best diagnostic tool for motor neurone disease was an electromagnetic test of her nerve responses (an EMT) and there was a three-month wait for that too.

Marilyn now had immense difficulty walking, couldn't drive and was scared of stairs. She was fearful of falling, even when she was walking across a clear carpeted floor. She needed to be sure that she always had something to hold on to. We discussed it and we did not discuss it. Everyone was too terrified to express their true feelings. Did looking up motor neurone disease on the internet make it more likely that she had it?

I tried to find out about the fabled neurologist Dr D who was so busy that there appeared to be no real difference between his private or his NHS waiting list. I discovered his personal email and wrote to him in desperation, but this had no effect. We would have to wait. It would be 'foolish', he said, to rush into this.

Foolish.

Marilyn was getting worse by the day, and it seemed we could not see any specialist in Scotland or get a diagnosis at all. It had been three months since she first 'presented', and six months since the first fall. Now there was the possibility of a pandemic, although no one talked about that much either. It was only in Italy and China. It wasn't going to affect people in Britain too much, was it?

Ali phoned to check how things were going. 'For God's sake,' she said. 'Come down to London while you still can. I can find you a neurologist in twenty-four hours.'

And so, at the end of February 2020, as the signs first appeared in GPs' surgeries and hospitals warning of the imminent Coronavirus, we boarded the train to London and found ourselves in Queen Square talking to a charming doctor – Nick – who ran through all the reflex testing that we had come to know by heart, before sending us next door to the London Hospital of Neurology for an

EMT. It was administered by a kind Estonian doctor, who apologised. 'This can be quite painful.'

We saw Ali who looked guarded and shocked and loving and resigned all at the same time. She said we had to stay on in London until they had the results. 'There's no point returning to Scotland if you're going to have to come back down again in a week. Just wait.'

We made another appointment with Dr Nick and he was charming but sheepish and told us that he wanted a second opinion. There was a very good man, another Nik but without the 'c'. He could see us the next day. When I googled his name, I saw that his main field of expertise was MND. Ali phoned to say that she was 'so sorry'. She had already been told, of course, but even then, I couldn't quite believe this was happening. I heard the sadness in her voice.

Perhaps if I refused to accept it then it would disappear?

So, when we went to see Dr Nik without the 'c', we were given to understand that this was a formality, as if we already knew but it hadn't quite been spelt out. He looked at the EMT result, did the briefest of reflex tests ('Do you have to?' Marilyn asked) and then confirmed the diagnosis without, it seemed, quite mentioning the disease.

'How did I get it?' said Marilyn, as if there was something, anything, she could have done to avoid it: more exercise, more vitamin D, not being born in Scotland – a country where, along with multiple sclerosis, MND seems to be more prevalent (one report suggests that its incidence is 67 per cent higher in Scotland than in other Northern European countries).

'We don't know,' Dr Nik replied. 'But I can tell you that the people in Edinburgh are very good. You will be well looked after.'

'If we ever meet them,' I said.

'Oh, you'll see them now,' he assured us. 'I'll write to them. In fact, I'd like to dictate the letter in front of you so that you know what I am saying and can correct any errors. We'll get it off today. Is that all right?'

Was that all right? We didn't have much of a choice.

And so, we watched and listened as he spoke into his Dictaphone. Neither of us could quite believe that this was happening, that we were in this room, and there was nothing we could do. Our luck, our good fortune, our happiness, whatever you liked to call it, had run out at last and forever. There was no future to look forward to any more: only the fled past and a frightening present.

This is what Dr Nik dictated:

'Marilyn is a 72-year-old lady with no significant medical past. For the last six months she has fallen a number of times and has noticed that her hands are significantly weaker. Marilyn works as a director of audio and theatre and she is unable to maintain her voice as normal. She is unable to sing.'

Marilyn looked at me. I held her hand. She held mine. Was this the end of us? We returned to the doctor and his dictation.

'On examination she clearly found it difficult to get up from her chair. Whistling was more challenging. The tongue appeared to be normal.

'There is a suggestion of weakness of head flexion (4+/5).'

[What did this mean?]

'In the upper limb there was wasting and weakness, distally more so on the left (FDI 4-/5).'

[What was FDI? Later I looked it up. First dorsal interosseous.]

'Bedside testing of power in the lower limb was unremarkable.'

['It would have been remarkable if I'd been doing it,' I said, trying to be funny, because it was so awful.]

'I reviewed the investigations including EMG. Unfortunately, the history and examination are consistent with MND. We spoke at length about the diagnosis. It is a highly variable disorder which makes predicting prognosis futile ...'

Futile.

We listened as he concluded, shook our hands, put on his bicycle clips and wished us well. He couldn't have been any nicer. It's just that the words were all wrong.

We took the train home and Marilyn said, 'It's strange. I will never see London again.'

We texted the girls, Marilyn's sister, my sister. I had given up alcohol, but I had two beers. It was late at night. Rosie met us at the station with a kind and cheerful guard from LNER who had a station wheelchair and a taxi waiting.

We went home and drank tea. Ali phoned again. She told us that the Covid situation was going to get a lot worse. We should see our closest friends as soon as we could.

The next morning, Marilyn dictated an email:

I wanted to let you know that yesterday, after a barrage of tests and scans, they have diagnosed that I have motor neurone disease. At the moment I feel fit and well though I tire quite easily and I sound and walk like Margaret Rutherford on a bad day. Rest assured that I am still very much on email, though talking on the phone is tricky; and I am still working away on various projects.

As you can imagine, we are still in the early stages of processing this news, and I am spending all my time with

James, Rosie, Charlotte, Sean and Bea. You can still email me,
or even better James, but please understand if we don't reply
speedily.

 With much love
 Marilyn

We realised that we would now have to embark on a
crash course in the disease; rather like doing a university
degree you had never intended to sign up for, or being
involved in a play in a language you couldn't speak that
should never have been staged in the first place.

There was one question we still had to ask Ali.

'How long have we got?'

'It's impossible to say. Every case is different; but you can
look up the average.'

Motor neurone disease is called 'the thousand-day
disease', because that's the average life expectancy after
diagnosis. However, this diagnosis seemed to have taken
ages, and what were we going to count as the first
symptoms? The pain at Gladstone's Library? The first fall
at the concert?

'Two years?' I asked.

'If you're lucky,' said Ali.

'That seems a long time, given how she is now.'

'I know.'

'It says six months to two years. Could it be as short as
six months?'

'If you're lucky,' Ali said again, meaning that brevity
would at least cut short the distress. 'It's horrible. I am so
sorry.'

In the end, it was five months and twenty-two days.

Before …

How We Met

In 1983, I was working as a producer in the BBC Radio Drama Script Unit in London on a non-renewable fixed-term contract. I was twenty-four years old. If I wanted to stay in the Corporation when it came to an end, I would have to find another job within it. There were three possibilities: one in Belfast, one in Birmingham and then a one-year 'attachment' (the irony is not lost on me now) in Edinburgh. One of the three radio drama producers there, a woman called Marilyn Imrie, was going to work as a script editor in television for a year and they needed someone to replace her. Because my grandfather was Scottish, and because I loved the festival and the city, I thought that the only non-permanent job, in Edinburgh, was the best option and, if it didn't work out, I would just come back to London.

I had never met Marilyn properly before, but we had sat next to each other on a sofa in a BBC script meeting. I had been struck by how extraordinarily pale she was. She had the gentlest and warmest of voices and she smelled of hyacinth, jasmine and coriander, the perfume I later came to know as Mystère de Rochas. She had just produced David Rudkin's *Ashes* and Jessie Kesson's *The White Bird*

Passes and won an award for Trisha Fine's play *Can You Hear Me?* She had come down to London from Edinburgh to secure commissions for plays by Bernard MacLaverty and Liz Lochhead and discuss her plans for an adaptation of Robert Louis Stevenson's *Kidnapped*. Because the room was full and crowded, we never actually spoke to one another.

'Who was that pale woman?' I asked my boss afterwards.

'Why? Are you interested?'

'No, it's just that ... her skin is like milk.'

'She's been through a lot. Perhaps it's what makes her a good director.'

'Do you need to be unhappy to direct?' I wondered.

I was talking to Ronald Mason, a generous hard-drinking chain-smoker from Belfast who had been Head of Programming in Northern Ireland at the start of the Troubles. He had incredibly elegant fingers and he wore a crisp, perfectly ironed white shirt with a lemon-yellow tie and gold cufflinks. He looked like a benevolent gangster who spent his free time reading Yeats.

'You need to understand desperation,' he said, as if this was the most obvious thing in the world.

(When Marilyn and I married, he gave us a black marble rolling pin with the injunction: 'Not to be used in disputes.')

A year later, after I had got the job and arrived in Edinburgh, my new boss thought it would be a good idea if we all met together to have a bit of a lunch and, this being the 1980s, 'a bit of a lunch' meant a nice restaurant, gin and tonics, a lot of wine and not much work afterwards, especially for men who didn't have to worry too much about childcare.

It was just before Easter. Marilyn was very late, she always was in those days, and arrived at Black's Restaurant in Jeffrey Street, in a red summer coat over a black-and-white gingham dress, with a chunky fake pearl necklace and matching earrings. I stood up as she arrived (I had been well brought up) and she came over, smiled, and kissed me hello.

'You sat next to me on that grey sofa. I remember. Shall we sit next to each other now? I can let you in on all the things they won't have dared to tell you.'

Who is this extraordinary woman? I thought, astonished by the velocity of her character and the enveloping warmth of her presence. And then, almost immediately: I wonder if she has a boyfriend?

She was eleven years older than me, divorced, and living as a single mother with Rosie, her five-year-old daughter from a subsequent relationship. She told me that she had 'completely given up on men', but I could phone her for a chat about work any time and we could, perhaps, go to a film sometime, although it was hard for her to get a babysitter when she was already commuting to Glasgow every day.

'I'll babysit,' I said.

'You don't mean that.'

'I do. I hardly know anyone here. How else am I going to fill my time?'

'I'll have to get to know you a bit better first.'

'Well, let's go to a film, then.'

Marilyn chose *Rumble Fish*, Francis Ford Coppola's now cult American Noir film about boy gangs in Tulsa, Oklahoma, starring Matt Dillon, Mickey Rourke, Dennis Hopper, Nicolas Cage and Diane Lane. For anyone at all interested in pursuing a career in film or television this was essential viewing. Shot principally in black and white, it combines French New Wave freshness with German expressionist lighting techniques and *Koyaanisqatsi*-style time-lapse. It also features a soundtrack by Stewart Copeland from the Police. This was just the kind of thing any would-be cineaste should be watching, and I had form on this, having been chucked by my girlfriend Mary in the middle of Tarkovsky's *Mirror* in the Hampstead Everyman.

Now, however, sitting next to this lovely woman and watching what seemed to me to be a piece of self-indulgent nonsense, even by Francis Ford Coppola's standards, I wanted to walk out. This was going to be ninety-four minutes in the cinema when I could have been talking to Marilyn. She didn't have the endless free time of youth. She needed to pack in a film that she could talk about at work and get back to the midweek babysitter for ten o'clock.

'Are you enjoying this?' I whispered, as a black-and-white Mickey Rourke was mesmerised by a full-colour Siamese fighting fish in an Oklahoma pet shop.

'I think it's really interesting. Are you not?'

'I'd rather be with you.'

'I never walk out of films,' she replied, but noticing my restlessness after all the pets in the pet shop had been set free and I had let out an audible 'Oh, for God's sake', Marilyn agreed to leave. We went into Dario's Pizza in the Lothian Road for a Four Seasons and a bottle of Valpolicella. I explained why I had hated the film and she told me how I had missed the point. In the rom-com of our lives, I suppose this would count as the first argument.

I was grumpy, I told her, not just about the film and the limited time we had together, but also because there was so little to do at work. There was no radio drama to be made until I had commissioned a few writers, and no one seemed to be in any particular hurry to get on with anything. I was encouraged to 'use the time to think creatively' and so I told Marilyn that I was toying with the idea of directing some Chekhov in the theatre.

'*The Cherry Orchard* is my favourite play.'

'I want to do *Three Sisters*.'

'Why?'

She leant forward, curious about the possibility, clearly interested in the opportunity to discuss how such a production might proceed. It was a look of hers that I later came to love and adore, the look of expectation, intrigue, the beginning of something new. Filled with the confidence of youth, I set out my plans for the show, oblivious to the irony of my mansplaining feminine frustration and marital disappointment to the experienced woman opposite.

I told her that I thought the play was about ignorance and limitations of privilege, how all of the characters apart from the maid and the army doctor assume that the action is about them. They think they have been marked out for something special, and it takes them the course of the play to realise that they have not. They are as susceptible to the quiet desperation of everyday lives as anyone else. I wanted to think of ways in which self-centred individuals, concentrating too much on their own ambition, were brought to a place where a beautiful melancholy could be the beginning of hope. Marilyn smiled and said, 'Go on.'

I did, for far too long, and then she told me how important she thought it was to make the world off-stage as convincing as what happens on it: the fire in the town, the soldiers marching, the duel between Tuzenbach and Soliony. We have to want to go to Moscow as badly as the Three Sisters; just as we hear the music across the lake at the beginning of *The Seagull*. We imagine the beauty of *The Cherry Orchard* even if we cannot see it, we can't bear for it to be chopped down, and we have to understand how hard it is for the family to return to their old home and how desperate is their melancholy when they leave it for the last time: 'Goodbye old house, goodbye old life!'

Marilyn said that when she had been very sad, the previous year, and 'couldn't stay cheerful any longer', her daughter Rosie wanted to make her feel better. 'What's your favourite play?' she asked, and then performed her own version of what she thought *The Cherry Orchard* might be like with her dolls, her toys and her puppets.

And so there we were, eating pizza and using Chekhov to talk about the comedy and pathos of everyday life, the desire of the characters to be more than they were, the disappointments of those who felt that life had passed them by, and how to make the future a realistic possibility rather than a dream.

A week later Marilyn phoned up and asked, 'Did you mean what you said about babysitting? I'm really stuck.'

'I'll do it,' I said and came to a spacious ground-floor flat in Craigmillar Park where I was introduced to Rosie, her equally pale and even more suspicious daughter. I think we read stories and watched some television and Rosie showed me a wooden chair that had been bound with red-and-white ribbons, odd bits of material, rope and string.

How I came to be tied to this chair, I cannot fully remember, apart from Rosie saying, 'You're my prisoner,' but by the time Marilyn came home I was still stuck, even though I could easily get out, because I didn't want to let Rosie down and because I thought it would amuse Marilyn.

'Well, that's one way of getting a man to stay,' she said when she returned, 'but I'm still sworn off them.'

Over the next few weeks, we saw each other several times. I made what I thought was my famous minestrone soup, as if no one had ever made such a thing before, and brought it round to her house where we talked even more about my profit-share production of *Three Sisters*. It was going to be staged at the Netherbow in the Royal Mile.

Although I had been to drama school and was youthfully confident about my directing, this had all been in England with actors who were used to doing a lot of talking about Peter Brook and Stanislavski, arc and action, method and motivation. Scottish actors were more instinctive and impatient. They weren't so interested in poetic understanding or the writer's intention. Their preparation was more visceral. Perhaps there was more of the tradition of variety and the music hall in their DNA.

I was reminded of a teacher at drama school who kept repeating the phrase: 'It's SHOW-business, not TELL-business, darling.' These Scottish actors wanted to act with their bodies as well as their heads. They preferred to stand up and get on with it rather than sit around discussing the difference between intention and action.

Whenever I tried to 'do a bit of directing' or give a note, I was met with the response: 'I thought I was doing that.'

One of them told me about the actor John Stahl, who, after listening to twenty minutes of notes from an English director on how he should deliver a line, replied, 'I'll do it with a look.'

After one of the (male) actors said to me, 'I don't do vulnerability,' I phoned Marilyn to ask for tips. She told me about the need to be clear and patient and let the actors find their way. 'Don't think you have to give them all the answers.'

'But I feel like I'm failing them.'

'It's a process. You've got three weeks. You have to let things bed down.'

'The only thing I want to bed down—'

'Yes, yes, that's quite enough of that.'

In the end I learned so much from the actors, not just about the play and the art of performance but what it might mean to live in Scotland and how it was a different country inside Mrs Thatcher's Britain. They said what they thought, were warm and challenging, and I came to understand what some people in Glasgow call their 'aggressive friendliness'. They didn't like bullshit, they couldn't stand pretension, they wanted to be loved (don't we all?) and they wanted a laugh and a drink and to be paid on time.

And then I realised that this was not just another production. It was a crash-course degree in how to behave in Scotland, a lesson in how generous and creative people in a different country think, and it was the best accidental preparation I could have had for loving Marilyn.

I continued to talk to her, and she said that the designer and I could come round to her flat after the technical rehearsal and turn our anxieties into excitement over a bottle of red wine. Kevin and I went over to Craigmillar Park and told her all our hilarious and extraordinary anecdotes about the amazing time we were having. Marilyn listened to us *two boys* as if she had never heard such stories in her life, even though she had been married to a theatre director for five years and seemed to know every performer in Scotland.

On the day of the first night, she sent me a telegram to wish me good luck: YOU SAY IRENA AND I SAY IRENA. DON'T CALL THE WHOLE THING OFF!

That evening she sat next to the theatre critic of the *Scotsman*. 'Don't worry,' she said to me, 'I'll see her right.'

The next day I received a card promising that she had loved the production. It was a pen-and-ink cartoon 'Biff Kard', satirising the *Guardian*-reader set, entitled 'How to Behave at a Preview', with a louche John Grierson film director lookalike holding a dry martini and saying, 'This is my masterpiece – hand and glass locked in a tension of opposites,' and his glamorous date replying, 'Don't be a wally, Nigel. People will hear you.'

Marilyn had added extra speech bubbles. The one at the top read: 'It certainly has all the hallmarks of genuine Runcie ... but is it Chekhov?'

And at the bottom: 'It certainly has all the hallmarks of Chekhov ... but is it authentic Runcie?'

She signed the card: 'With love as always'.

Always. I had only known her a few months. I started a notebook and began to write down all my thoughts about her, little memories, hopes and anxieties, and copied out Masha's confession in *Three Sisters*: 'I'm in love – all right, so that's my fate. So that's my lot in life. Somehow, we shall live our lives, whatever happens to us. You read some novel and you think, that's all so trite and obvious. But as soon as you fall in love yourself, you realise that no one knows anything, and that we each have to decide these things for ourselves.'

All my friends had assumed that, if I was ever going to marry, it would either be to some posh English girl (I had recently been to a Wodehousian wedding where I had sat between two women called Arabella Harcourt-Seeley and Jamanda Haddock) or to some scarily neurotic actress with a vodka problem. My most recent relationship had ended with an upturned bowl of spaghetti in my lap and a postcard with a razor blade sellotaped to it explaining what I should do to my penis. I should probably add that at this time my father was also the Archbishop of Canterbury and the idea of my marrying a woman who was eleven years older than me, a divorced single parent with a five-year-old daughter, would have sent my parents into a bit of a spin.

Marilyn took me in her yellow Citroën 2CV down to Skippers Bistro in Leith and we sat at a shared table so we couldn't speak as privately as I wanted to, and she showed me how to eat lobster properly. She had learned how to do so in France, and I wondered what on earth I could do to get this woman, who was dressed in what appeared to be a grey silk flying suit, to spend more time with me.

I told her that my favourite writer was Henry James and she replied, saying that she preferred Robert Louis Stevenson. Henry James 'always chewed more than he bit off'.

When I said that I was going to do a Scottish production of Strindberg's *Miss Julie* for Radio 3, she sent me a hand-drawn cartoon of a watching budgerigar saying: 'Jings! Whit's Jock daein' wi' thon chopper?'

Then I received a postcard from her, a painting by Phryne Frappa of a woman unveiling in front of three eager old men, with the words: 'Three elderly producers inspecting my credentials before joining Radio Drama – don't you love it?'

She left a box of rose-hip tea in my doorway.

Dearest James
This box of tea

Is spent with special love
From me.

She said she didn't want to ruin me (although I was perfectly prepared to be ruined if it meant being with her). It wasn't fair on either of us. She insisted over the next ten days that there was *absolutely no chance of a relationship*. We were friends. She encouraged me to 'find a proper girlfriend' and she would vet her for bonkersness, and I did manage, quite soon, too soon probably, to spend some time with a petite and extraordinarily attractive chain-smoking ballerina. We sat in gloomy pubs, even at the height of summer, with very little to say to each other and stayed in weekend getaway hotels with yellow nylon sheets and drank in pointless golf and tartan-styled lounge bars in St Andrews with me thinking, alternately, 'Shit, it's still only eight o'clock' and 'I wish I was with Marilyn.' I realise this does not put me in a particularly good light, but then I think the ballerina was only dating me to get her old boyfriend back which, in the end, she succeeded in doing.

Before returning for a production that I had to do in London, I dropped round a little toy that I had bought in Jenners department store for Rosie's sixth birthday. I arrived, not thinking, in the middle of her birthday party and left straight away. Marilyn sent me a note on red paper waiting for my return:

Welcome home James!
(a red-letter day!)
Hope studios, travels and sojourns were all smooth and pleasant. Craigmillar Park enterprises await your return for your participation in jolly summer jaunts — ring for details!

*Please forgive my erratic and (I'm sure) seemingly
thoughtless behaviour at times over the last few weeks. Life's a
bit too bumpy for comfort – but I hope you and I are going to
be friends. I look forward to it.*

With love, Marilyn

*PS. The lion continues to be much loved. It was so kind
of you ...*

At the Edinburgh Festival that year she had so many
people staying that it was almost impossible to see her, but
she phoned me up and said she had an afternoon free and
was desperate to escape. Would I like to go with her to the
Creation exhibition at the Gallery of Modern Art?

This was, perhaps, one of the first shows to concentrate
on environmental perception. It was about the human
position in space, time and landscape, with areas devoted
to The Beginning, The Heavens, The Earth, The Seas,
The Planets, The Creatures and The Human Image: seven
sections for the seven days of Creation.

Marilyn was tired and told me that all she wanted was
quiet and beauty and space and company. It was a hot
afternoon but the galleries were not crowded, and we
walked between paintings before sitting down on a low
bench in front of Emil Nolde's *Large Poppies (red, red, red)*
from 1942, one of the few pictures he was able to paint
in the Nazi period: a big, blowsy image of deep crimson,
scarlet and mauve poppies at the height of summer in
what looked to be a strong wind.

I had bought the catalogue and read from Nolde's
autobiography: 'The blossoming colours of the flowers and
the purity of those colours – I love them. I loved the flowers
and their fate: shooting up, blooming, radiating, glowing,
gladdening, bending, wilting, thrown away and dying.'

'Gladdening,' said Marilyn thoughtfully. 'They cheer my heart.'

She talked about wild poppies growing in the hedgerows of Fife, of her childhood and the country lanes and the sea at St Andrews. Then she stopped talking and we just sat there. I think something extraordinary then happened that we acknowledged but couldn't quite explain. It was a resting place, a coming-in to land, a feeling of security and companionship. This was where we were. We could stop here for a while without saying anything. It was a feeling of having come home. I knew then, more than ever, that this was all I needed, to be with this person at this time. Love need not be desperate or hasty, it could just be warm, tacit, accepting; the feeling I would later recognise when love was described as 'being with someone you can do nothing with'.

I do not know how long we sat there, but I think it was longer than I had ever sat in front of any other painting. I knew that neither of us wanted to leave, that love was a form of rescue and we had somehow saved each other from all our present anxieties if only for a short while in that time and space; and that, whenever we were nervous or anxious about each other in the future, we could come back to this moment when we were alone and together. Then, God willing, there would be other such moments, perhaps, over the future years, where we would know each other without speaking, and understand that no one and nothing else mattered.

But Marilyn was worried by what we had started and how everything was going to turn out. She wasn't sure if it was fair on me. Surely, I was too young? Perhaps she should let me go like the Marschallin does with her young lover in Strauss's *Rosenkavalier*. Did I know it? (No, of course I didn't.)

I refused to listen and said that I was only interested in her and she said, 'What about the ballerina?' and I said, 'You know that's hopeless. Even she thinks it's hopeless. We're both on the rebound.'

Then Marilyn and I went away from the bench in front of a painting of poppies in full flower and buffeted by the wind, back to our normal everyday jobs as if we too were characters from *Three Sisters* forced to come to terms with the fact that we had boring mundane everyday lives just like everybody else.

Except that we refused to accept this. I sent jaunty messages to Marilyn, basically saying HELLO! I AM HERE.

She came into the Radio Drama office over the weekend and wrote a little note on the back of a postcard of a Hugh Cameron painting called *A Lonely Life* and added: '*Sans toi, chéri, certainement!* The sun is pouring into my/your/our office this morning and I feel the need of your company.' Beneath, she added a riddle:

My first is in Jam but not in honey
My second is in rain but not in sunny
My third is in mine but not in yours
My fourth is in below and in above
My last is in kisses
It's you that I love.

And then, upside down at the bottom, just in case I hadn't understood, she wrote: 'Is James the answer?'

If we didn't see each other, we sent one another cards and letters and internal BBC memos with 'Private' scrawled across the back of the envelopes. I found out that her middle name was Elsie and that two of her female friends called her 'Marilyn Elsie Fatbottom'.

Then I received another riddle:

My first is in beetle
But never in ant
My second's in flower
But not in plant
My third is in tipple
But not in drink
My fourth is in tap
But not in the sink
My fifth is in orange but not in plum
My sixth is in mine
In short it's my …?
And this object, which is animal, vegetable and mineral, longs
    to be close to yours
Ever your own daft Elsie
Kisses on the bottom xxx

I told her I couldn't wait for us to be together, and she promised me: 'Everything will change soon. I have so many fears, insecurities and anxieties, but none of them are about you and me. I believe that we were meant to find each other.'

She went on yet another course, away at BBC Elstree, and I gave her a bottle of Mystère de Rochas and phoned to say that I would miss her and longed for her return. All I wanted was to see her again.

So, I had to wait for her and realised that love was as much about patience as anything else. At the same time I knew, instinctively and absolutely, that I had no choice because this was the woman I loved and wanted to be with at whatever cost. It wasn't a *coup de foudre*. It was worth everything. Marilyn was going to define my life.

However, I still had to earn her trust. I had to show that I cared passionately and, at the same time, demonstrate that I was ready to wait. I had to prove my love to a woman who said she no longer had faith in men, love or marriage; and yet, simultaneously, we had to make sure that we didn't analyse everything too much or go over things in a way that would destroy the unpredictability, the informality and the excitement of all that was possible. We had to learn all the lessons that the Three Sisters hadn't.

There was so much to say and yet it was also simple. We loved each other, whatever the difficulties that might lie ahead. We had to believe and trust that this was true. Christians talk about a leap of faith. We had to hold hands and jump without looking down, but both of us couldn't help but peek through the hands over our eyes and think: Oh God, what an abyss.

We spoke on the phone when she was on her course in London and acknowledged both that it was almost impossible and that we missed each other madly. I told her that I couldn't imagine a life without her, such a thing was inconceivable now, but perhaps we didn't have to do *everything* straight away. Maybe we could just make a start?

Marilyn told me that she had met up with her friend Liz, who had told her not to get in a state. 'Why are you making such a fuss? Just have a wee affair. You don't have to marry him.'

Then I got this message: *I think you are a wonderful and extraordinary man – the warmest I have ever known. I want you to believe how happy you make me – it's like being given a present of something you thought you'd lost. Also, the thing is, I fancy you rotten. Can anything be done about this?*

She told me that she was getting the sleeper back from London. She knew that she would be exhausted and would need a rest as she never slept well on the train, but I could come round on Saturday afternoon. Rosie was staying with her grandparents in Fife. Could I just pop round and see her?

I brought her jonquils and honey and she opened the door and was so sleepy that, for a moment, I thought she had forgotten that I was coming, but then she smiled and made Earl Grey tea in her black velvet dressing gown with nothing underneath and said, 'Oh for goodness' sake, come to bed.'

And that was how it began.

Death as Theatre

> Anyone who made the marriage vow 'in sickness and in health', however sincerely meant, would never have been able to envisage that a disease such as MND would transform their world.
>
> Kevin Talbot and Rachael Marsden, *Motor Neuron Disease: The Facts*

Terminal illness is a full-time job. Given our background, the only way the family knew how to approach it was as some kind of weird and unexpected new production.

In the theatre, everything moves with gathering intensity towards the first night. Get that right, and you can refine and adapt and change as the run goes on. But we were working towards a last night, at an unspecified date, for one performance only.

Marilyn had taught us that the qualities necessary for any production were preparation, adaptability and holding your nerve. She was the calmest and most serene of directors, believing that anxiety was contagious. Her approach was to create a generous and inclusive atmosphere in which everyone could be at their best.

But what was this impromptu, unscheduled and unscripted production going to be like when she was not in charge and was undoubtedly going to be at her worst?

Soon, she would be unable to issue instructions or explain what she wanted, because her speech was disappearing almost as fast as her energy, hope and enthusiasm.

Her shows often began with the excitement of combining an idea and an author. She spent hours making sure that the building blocks of a production were right. Each scene had to progress the action and every character had to have a purpose, an arc and a direction. There had to be light and shade between main plot, character plot and all the little subplots. There needed to be opportunities for surprise and reversals (where, just as you think everything is going swimmingly, there is a dramatic shift for the worse). And then you had to knit it all together and make sure that no one in the audience could see the joins. Her job as a director was to provide a safe and creative framework in which everyone could feel secure without being constricted. She chose her music early, wanting to find the rhythm of the drama, believing that although some productions contained terrific moments, they couldn't always sustain their momentum.

'Lots of people can direct scenes, but they can't direct plays, James. It's not just about the good bits. It's about the piece as a whole. Everything has to be earned and paid off. Then you add the grace notes.'

Some plays might come with an existing character: *The Stanley Baxter Playhouse* for Radio 4, or John Mortimer's *Rumpole* with Benedict Cumberbatch and then Julian Rhind-Tutt. Or, it might start with an actor and an idea. The last production we did together was the aforementioned *Tap Dancing with Jean-Paul Sartre*. It started because our friend, the actor Ashley Smith, looks a little like Audrey Hepburn, and we wanted to find a vehicle for her. Marilyn had the idea that we could create something around the making of the film *Funny Face* with Fred Astaire. When we spoke about it together, I thought it would be fun to introduce Jean-Paul Sartre, on the principle that they could teach him about tap dancing and he could reveal the meaning of life at the same time. So, we started with the actor, the idea and the music ('It don't mean a thing if it ain't got that swing') and tried to be as playful as we could. It was entertainment, showbiz, joy and ridiculousness.

But this last production that we were forced into planning in real life without preparation or warning had none of these things. There was no script and we had no ideas about the casting. The first person we needed was a neurologist but, as previously discussed, Scotland's star neurologist had a waiting list of three months and so, as in the theatre, he 'wasn't available'. The company that had recently won an award for 'Scotland's Best Care Provider' was fully booked and wasn't taking on new patients. The Covid crisis meant that MND Scotland could not give us any physiotherapy or massage.

This was not a good start. But we were familiar with this kind of casting dilemma. You start by asking for Meryl Streep and work down.

So, we did finally manage to find a determined and helpful care company to provide two hours a day (leaving Rosie and me with the other twenty-two) while Charlotte was looking after her two-year-old daughter. She had no childcare and Covid had closed all the nurseries.

The carers that came were intrigued by our theatrical lifestyle.

'Have you worked with any famous actors?' one of them asked, and Marilyn nodded. 'Just a few.'

'Anyone I might have heard of?'

This is always a difficult question, because younger people want you to say Emma Watson and older people expect Laurence Olivier. None of them have actually 'heard' of the people you have actually worked with. Fame is not as extensive as we like to think. (I was reminded of David Sedaris's fine observation that people may be celebrities in this world, but what about the rest of the universe? All that vast space where no one knows them at all.)

During this production we had to work fast because it had started without us quite realising it had done so, as if we were filling in a slot that had become unexpectedly available. There was the feeling of accelerating panic that always accompanies an unprepared, underfunded and under-resourced production. There was no budget and no schedule, only a gradually accumulating cast of characters that came to resemble an eighteenth-century playbill.

The Reluctant Patient
A Tragic Farce in One Act

Dramatis Personae
Miss Marilyn Imrie, the Reluctant Patient
Mr James Runcie, her husband
Miss Rosie Kellagher, her eldest daughter
Miss Charlotte Runcie, her youngest daughter

Dr Ali Joy, friend of the above
Dr A–L, a Palliative Care Doctor
Dr R, a General Practitioner
Dr J, a Hospice Doctor
Miss A, an MND Nurse
Miss B, a Specialist in Ventilation
Miss L, a Speech Therapist
Miss S, a Social Carer
Miss K, a Physiotherapist

The Reverend Neil Gardner, a Minister

A Chorus of Carers: Anna, Fiona, Christie, Carol
Six District Nurses

Theatricals on the telephone (billed in alphabetical order to avoid dispute):
Miss Hetty Baynes
Miss Deborah Findlay
Mr Bill Paterson
Miss Siobhán Redmond
Miss Gerda Stevenson
Mr Pip Torrens

Characters at the corner shop, the dry-cleaner's and the pharmacy
Local friends and townsfolk

The action takes place in the City of Edinburgh and in the
village of St Monans.
In the midst of a plague.
The Year of Our Lord 2020.

Each of the medical characters had their own specialist skills. The trick was going to be to get them all to work together in a unified and coordinated production. Unfortunately, they didn't appear to know how to do this and, in a time of Covid, they were unable to see Marilyn in person.

This was not so much a play but a series of variety acts. We were also in the wrong venue. Our Edinburgh home had a bathroom and toilet that could not accommodate a wheelchair, the entrance to the bedroom was too narrow and there were awkwardly deep steps up to the front door. The possibility of adapting our flat to enable the best care was compromised by a Covid lockdown that prevented builders, carpenters and electricians coming into our home at all. At the same time, the acceleration of MND made the production 'schedule' tighter and tighter.

There was no designer, no stage manager, no prop master. New equipment was delivered to the door and we had no idea how to install or use it (and some of it didn't work). Rosie and I manipulated bath boards, bath chairs and walking frames; steps, ramps, rests, cushions and pillows; specialist cutlery, drinking cups and food blenders. Ventilators and nebulisers arrived and, although an utterly magnificent woman called Angela showed us how to use them, we had to keep checking the instruction manual and going online to find a way of nursing by YouTube.

Everything came to us at speed. There was hardly time to learn how each piece of kit worked before the pace of the illness made most of the props redundant within two weeks of their arrival.

In the early days, it seemed that we were involved in the bleakest of bedroom farces. Some of the actors weren't up to the job. Out of the first group of carers, lovely though they were, one didn't know how to support Marilyn as she still tried, vainly, to walk; another hadn't changed bedlinen before; a third did not know how to tie shoelaces. When a fourth told us that she couldn't take out Marilyn's earrings, because she had 'a thing' about 'anything that's been in the body', I phoned the organisation to tell them that this wasn't good enough. As a result, I was put through to the woman who ran it.

'Ah yes,' she explained, 'Jane's got a fetish about piercing.'

'You mean a phobia?'

'No, I mean a fetish.'

'I don't think you do.'

'We all have them, Mr Runcie. I've got one about belly buttons. In my early days, when I was caring myself, if I had to wash a patient, I could never catch a sight of their belly button. One glance and I was off. Thought I was going to be sick. Some people are funny like that, aren't they?'

I wanted to give her a badge, as I secretly planned to hand out to so many people over the coming months, saying: *This is not about you.*

That would have been mean. But I didn't know what I was doing any more. Illness makes you mad. It takes you into the opposite of a 'brave new world'. It is a stage on which you hoped you might never have to play a part and in which there is a savage, unreal humour. Our friend Anna told me that, after chemotherapy and the loss of her hair, she went to her local fishmonger who looked at her shaved head and said, 'Hello, Anna, haven't seen you for a bit. Fashion or cancer?'

Our production started running out of control from the very first week of 'rehearsals'. We changed our care provider and chucked more people and more money at the problem in an attempt to 'save the show' but this particular production was unsalvageable. As our GP, Dr R, told us: 'You just have to keep going but, in the end, there is nothing you can do. You have to give in. It just overwhelms you.'

Rosie moved the set around (the main sitting room) and tried to make backstage (the bedroom) as comfortable as possible. There was new furniture (an electric rise-and-recline mobility chair) and different lighting (candles). The initial design had developed into a site-specific show with no audience: or rather, an audience of one or two people at a time.

On Midsummer's Day we decided to visit St Monans. By this stage, travelling anywhere involved packing as if we were going on a family holiday. The car was filled with hospital equipment, walking aids, a ramp and a wheelchair. Getting in and out of it without a fall or some other accident was terrifying. Every movement required extreme concentration.

As we finally set off, the whole business of leaving the house having taken far longer than any of us had anticipated, each of us was thinking, Why are we doing this? Is it really worth the effort? After ten minutes on the road, Rosie insisted that we turn back. We had forgotten Marilyn's neck support and she could not manage the trip without it.

For God's sake, I thought as the journey elongated and felt even more futile.

But we arrived to a clear blue sky, no wind, calm seas and a light that felt as if it would never dim. There were so few people about we seemed to have the entire village to ourselves. It was a still point in a turning world, a time of calm and beauty in which, just for a moment, we could forget that Marilyn was ill. She asked to go to the far end of the harbour where we stopped to look back at the picture-postcard beauty of the houses on the shore. It was the perfect stage set.

Marilyn smiled. She was happy. Joy was still possible. Pleasure was still possible. We were at home on a flawless Scottish evening and none of us had any desire to be anywhere else. We did not want the day to end, determined to wring out every drop of bliss.

It was her last delight.

The following morning was dull and grey. It was spitting with rain. As Rosie helped her out of her chair, Marilyn froze, unable to walk, stand or support herself. Overnight, the illness had moved on to its next relentless stage. If the previous day had been like a dream dress rehearsal, now we could feel the curtain coming down. No more midsummer light, no more beauty, no more smiles, no more laughter, no more loveliness. *Finita la commedia*.

Even then, Marilyn tried to cheer us up, because that was who she was, always seeking out the positive, adding the grace notes, squeezing out the last pips of joy, knowing that life can be ridiculous even when it is at its most tragic. That evening, we watched television and the news reported that, because of the pandemic, the Paralympics were going to be postponed.

'Good,' she said loudly. 'Another year to prepare.'

She always had a fantastic sense of the larky and the ludicrous. When we were then introduced to the concept of a hoist to lift her from place to place and the carers told her that it was going to be quite difficult, Marilyn replied, 'Don't worry. I used to be a glider pilot.'

This was something I didn't know. She had done this in her early twenties. She closed her eyes as she was lifted into the air as if she was in an immersive production of *Peter*

Pan, and I wondered if she was remembering gliding over the fields and farms of Fife, being in another place, a more exciting world, a theatrical or filmic dream: anywhere that was not stuck within the inexorable mundanity of a terminal illness.

Our friend Siobhán told me that the last act in a play is always the least rehearsed and here we were, encountering a surreal version of the same thing, the actor's nightmare of going onstage without knowing the lines, or being unable to remember the play they were actually *in*.

Just as with a first night in the theatre, there were the cards and the flowers and the messages of goodwill. After the show there would be all the questions about 'how it went'. And then, after the one and only night of this particular and exclusive one-woman show, there would be 'the get-out' and the removal of all the props and furniture.

Marilyn and I spoke about her ideas for the funeral and the memorial service and all the actors and musicians she would like to take part and I realised that it was this that was going to be her final production. It was something she could script and plan and control and it would be *her* production at last, not something that had been foisted on her like *The MND Show*.

She wrote to me:

Darling
   These are just some thoughts/suggestions for a possible future funeral/memorial service ... of course none of this may be at all possible in the current situation ... but you and the girls will decide and know best in the circumstances prevailing. I love you and totally trust that I will be delighted by whatever you arrange. You and the girls will know best.

I will be there in spirit
I promise faithfully.
MX

I couldn't really take this in, but this was her first draft of a service. It is, allegedly, one of the 'advantages' of a terminal illness. You have time to prepare.

My father did it when he had prostate cancer, writing his own memorial service and putting the script into a brown envelope called 'The Event'. He took great care over it and gave the script to me a few months before he died, saying, 'I'm rather looking forward to this.'

It's what we are all supposed to do in order to come to terms with our own mortality. We should, like stoics or medieval monks, imagine our own funeral, including the people we want to take part: the minister, the music, the friends and the readings. But very few of us do so, because we don't want to think about the end at all. It seems mawkish, sentimental, even self-indulgent, especially if you are not actually *dying* at the time. But now I think it's a good idea. And this was what was happening to us, all in a rush: this extra, unexpected, production. We could not shirk it. And we wanted it to be right.

When we talked about the idea of a ceremony, a funeral, a memorial or a show together, while Marilyn could still speak (we knew that it wouldn't be long before she could not talk at all) and with all the plans in front of us, she asked, rather tentatively, for something I had forgotten: the traditional, theatrical, 'final round' of applause.

'I will make sure that happens,' I said. 'People will do it anyway. Bill will start it off—' and, at that moment, I could not bear to imagine it.

It was going to be some show: the show of her life.

46

Venice

Marilyn had never been to Venice and so we decided to spend our honeymoon there. I knew the city well, having at one point wanted to become an art historian. When I was eighteen, I won an essay competition by writing about a Bellini altarpiece. The prize was a week's stay in the city, and I had already been back several times, drawn to its doomed magnificence, its floods and reflections, its mists and revelations. Here was a city that was like an ever-evolving stage set containing history, violence, romance, intrigue and despair. It made death and decay beautiful.

It was late November 1985. We stayed at the Hotel Luna Baglioni, just off St Mark's Square. On the first morning, we walked into the flooded Piazza San Marco, had a coffee at Caffè Florian and turned on to the seafront, passing the Doge's Palace and the Bridge of Sighs, until we reached the public gardens. When we looked back to the island of San Giorgio Maggiore and the Church of the Salute, it was midday. All the church bells started to ring. Marilyn said, 'I've never been so happy.'

We loved the theatricality of Venice. We spent a whole morning looking at a single room of Carpaccio paintings in San Giorgio degli Schiavoni. Marilyn drew her favourite details in her watercolour sketchbooks: a parrot nibbling at a lily, a fine greyhound, a patient little dog and an abandoned turban. We tried to imagine the music the trumpeters and drummers would be playing as St George brought back his slaughtered dragon for the approval of his patron. It was all colour, noise and sumptuous display. Later that day, the Venetians walking the streets for their evening *passeggiata* appeared to be the natural descendants of the characters in the paintings. We laughed to imagine what it might be like if people did this in Glasgow, as if they were performing their own local version of the walkdown in a Scottish pantomime, and Marilyn told me of a disastrous production of *Goodnight Vienna* in Paisley which had gone down 'about as well as a production of *Goodnight Paisley* would have gone down in Vienna'.

Four years later, when she was in labour for the birth of Charlotte, we remembered that morning walk out loud, imagining our steps to take the concentration away from the pain, and we knew then that we would always have this memory to return to; like the slip on two uneven flagstones that Proust makes at the end of *À la recherche du temps perdu* which brings all his memories flooding back, fills him with felicity and makes death indifferent to him.

Marilyn kept a notebook of everything we saw on our honeymoon. She had it specially bound and gilded by an Edinburgh bookbinder and gave it to me that Christmas:

Monday 25 November
We arrived in Venice in darkness, and a dark mist. Leaving the Hotel Luna, we walked to St Mark's Square and the moon shone down full and clear on to the Doge's Palace, the Campanile, the water and us. Some boys played football. The square and the sky were navy blue.

Wednesday 27 November
Today to the church of San Zaccaria – the saint who fathered John the Baptist. His remains rest here, and a perfect Bellini altarpiece of the Madonna with Saints (St Jerome in vivid red). As is common here, you insert 200 lira for light on your picture – after a short time you are plunged into darkness again: life!!

The Frari
Thursday afternoon
The Assumption of the Virgin by Titian. Set above the high altar is a piece of wonderful sumptuous craft. The vibrant orange clothed figure in the foreground, the Virgin's pink robe swirling around her, the blue of the sky below the gold of the heavens. Tonight, James gave me a silver butterfly brooch – farfallo. Delicate and perfect, like the time.

Our favourite place was the Ca' Rezzonico, and Marilyn writes of it as 'the most beautiful chilled marble, an icy palace of dead Poesy. Browning died here, and there is a play to be written about it, a film to be made, pictures to be painted!'

At the top of the building there are a series of pale and playful eighteenth-century frescoes by Giandomenico Tiepolo that tell the story of scenes from the life of Pulcinella, celebrating the joys of love, courtship and *commedia dell'arte*. Masked figures in white are walking on their hands, attempting a tightrope crossing or drinking and laughing after a game of badminton. It's a place of light, summer and celebration.

One scene, *The New World*, puts the viewer at the back of a crowd of people watching a puppetry act that we can't see.

'I love this,' Marilyn said. 'It's like waiting for the lights to go down in the theatre, the anticipation that you're going to be in for an adventure, a show in which anything might happen. Just like us.'

I realised that I was now looking at the world through her eyes as well as my own and that I wanted to develop and expand her thoughts in order to continue our conversation. This was the beginning of my wanting to become a writer. In fact, looking back now, I realise that I only became a novelist because of Marilyn. All my books have been dedicated to her. This is not just an act of thankfulness. It is an acknowledgement that she was the first person who made it possible for me to think imaginatively about what it might be like to be someone entirely different.

When we returned home from Venice, I tried to write a novel about the Ca' Rezzonico but I could never quite get it right. Instead, I wrote *The Colour of Heaven*, which begins with the discovery of an abandoned baby in a little side canal in the midst of the Ascension Day festivities. The boy is short-sighted, as I am, and he grows up to go on a journey along the Silk Route, in the spirit of Marco Polo, to search for the perfect ultramarine blue. He finds it in the lapis lazuli caves of Afghanistan, where he meets and falls in love with Aisha, a woman in her thirties who already has a child. So, in fact, it was all about Marilyn.

Venice became our romantic, imaginary home. It was the place where we knew that if we were ever lost or doubted each other we could go back and fall in love all over again. We planned to return every year until we were too old or incapacitated to do so. We even told the children that, when the time came, we wanted to have our ashes scattered over the lagoon.

Fifteen years into our marriage, and celebrating our anniversary, we arrived at Gatwick Airport and I asked Marilyn if she had remembered her passport. Exasperated, she told me that of course she had, here it was, and she opened it to see Charlotte's face staring back at her. 'Oh, my God, I've packed the wrong one.'

This could have cued up all manner of accusation but there was an evening flight from Luton with one space left on it, and we decided that I would travel ahead with the luggage, Marilyn would go home and pick up the correct passport and then come on later. I said I would meet her, just around midnight, at the Piazzale Roma, and we did just that, without any argument, and got the slow vaporetto with no one else on it down the Grand Canal, listening to the slap of the water, the grinding of the gears, and a lone gondolier singing the last of his songs under a full winter moon:

> 'o sole mio sta nfronte a te!
> 'o sole, 'o sole mio
> sta nfronte a te, sta nfronte a te!

His voice echoed against the old, indomitable stone. We listened as the boat moved through light and shadow. It was as if we were suspended in history. Marilyn cuddled into me and said, 'This is more romantic, isn't it? You see how it's all turned out for the best? Thank you for not being cross. Thank you for loving me.'

For her seventieth birthday, we took six friends and wandered through the rooms of the Ca' Rezzonico once more, sharing our secret favourite place. The next day, we went to the Locanda Cipriani on Torcello with Joanna and Richard, Jo and Stuart, Hildegard and Bill. We drank a crisp Verduzzo Amabile and ate fried courgette flowers and herb-scented grilled fish and talked of love and marriage and how much our friendship meant to each other. Marilyn laughed and laughed and encouraged Bill to tell one of his favourite anecdotes to get the party going. It was about Ken Dodd.

Following a gig in north-east Scotland, his friend Phil Cunningham, the great accordion-playing raconteur, was asked back to the manse by the local minister for a welcome gathering of the local great and the good. As he waited for his first drink of the evening, Phil couldn't help noticing a picture of Ken Dodd on the mantelpiece. He told the minister that he wouldn't normally have had him down as a fan of the buck-toothed Liverpudlian comic with the sticky-out hair. The host handed him his drink. When it was time for a refill, Phil tried again, talking of his love for Ken Dodd and his Diddymen. How tickled he was to have seen him in action. Surely the minister must have done so himself? Yet again, his host was reluctant to come clean. Still, Phil was determined to get the truth out. How did this man come to know Ken Dodd? It was only after his third enquiry, pointing to the picture on the mantelpiece yet again, that the minister grasped Phil's accordion-playing arm and said quietly but exceedingly firmly: 'That's my fucking wife.'

Marilyn had heard the story before but pretended not to have remembered it properly simply so that she could hear it again. She loved shared laughter and encouraging people to be their best selves. She knew the liberating freedom of true companionship where the cares of the world can disappear, if only for a while.

Afterwards we visited the Basilica of Santa Maria Assunta. The flooring was studded with stone and glass, designed in a swirl of cubes, semicircles and triangles that work as grounding to the most beautiful thirteenth-century Byzantine mosaics. We saw the Virgin Mary cradling the Christ Child. The gold background glimmered in the fading autumn light, as if lit by unseen candles, a shimmering glimpse of eternity.

We fell silent. Marilyn took my hand and we looked at an image of the Virgin in Glory filled with wisdom and grace. It had a knowledge of inevitability, but also a strange and lasting permanence. It was sure that it would always be there, long after we had all departed and died, waiting for the next visitors to be consoled by its serenity. We could have stayed there forever.

What Not to Say

Shortly after the diagnosis, a friend *who is a psychiatrist* told us that we should make sure we 'make the most of the precious time there is left'.

I told him that Marilyn and I didn't actually *need* a terminal illness to enjoy each other's company. *All* our time was precious. In another telephone call, he said that I could phone him 'whenever you like' but that 'Saturday afternoons are best for me'.

It's difficult to know what to say in these situations but I thought psychiatrists were supposed to be good at this sort of thing.

A friend in America emailed to say how shocked she was. She had a friend with MND in Bristol. Did I know him? Maybe she thought the diagnosis gave us access to its every victim.

Nurses with experiences of MND warned us that the disease was 'like a roller coaster' but, as the illness progressed, I thought, No, it's not. It's nothing like a roller coaster. Stop saying that. But all the professionals kept coming out with the same phrase, as if it were a mantra or a prayer or a way of filling the silence with a fact. 'Like a roller coaster'. Sometimes they added the word 'journey' for extra effect.

'The journey's like a roller coaster.'

'NO IT ISN'T,' I kept wanting to say. 'We're not going on a journey at all. We're stuck in this flat in Edinburgh in the middle of a lockdown. It is NOT A JOURNEY. And, more importantly, IT IS NOT A BLOODY ROLLER COASTER EITHER. With a roller coaster you have ups as well as downs. The ride is thrilling. With this disease there ARE NO UPS. It is down all the way and it is NEVER thrilling. Try to find some other metaphor. And, while you're at it, you might as well learn from us not to come out with such crap to your future patients.'

But I didn't ever say this. I just replied, 'Yes, I suppose it is.'

I sat on a sofa with the girls and said, 'If anyone tells us that we're going to come out of this stronger, I'm going to kill them.'

'MND,' said Rosie. 'The disease that brings families closer together.'

Dr R said, 'I'm sorry. You wouldn't wish this on your worst enemy.'

'Well, I don't know,' said Charlotte. 'I wouldn't rule it out. Maybe one day I'll meet someone really awful.'

If it was 'like' anything, it was similar to the myth of Sisyphus. No matter how far we pushed the stone up the hill it was always going to roll back down again.

Another friend, who is a therapist, sent me a text. *How are you?*

Three words that take under three seconds to write, requiring an answer that takes far longer. I have come to despise this phrase. There is an immediate answer. *Fine. Coping.* And there is a more hostile response too: *How the fuck do you think I am?*

What those caring for the sick need *least of all* is more work; more explanation, more *things to do*. To answer a friend's 'How are you?' takes time if you want to do it properly.

Almost as bad is 'I wish there was something I could do.'

Well unless you are prepared to help with the shopping, the feeding, the washing, there isn't anything really. I translated the phrase 'I wish there was something I could do' into 'There's nothing I can do' or even 'There's nothing I am prepared to do.'

All these remarks put the onus on the recipient.

Tip: 'Thinking of you' is better. As is 'Do not reply. Just to say that I know it must be impossible. I am sending all my love.'

Or this: 'James. Call any time if you want to, but not if you can't. Any time. Day or night. I mean it.'

Instead of Márquez's *Love in the Time of Cholera* we were faced with *Terminal Illness in the Time of Covid 19*. All our friends wanted to come and pay a visit but the one and only advantage of a pandemic was that we could legitimately say: 'No visitors.' Marilyn did not want to see anyone. She couldn't bear the idea of people witnessing her decline. She was determined to be remembered at her best. Furthermore, she didn't want to upset people. At the beginning of her illness, she could still send little texts and emails but speaking on the phone was hopeless. It exhausted her and she ran out of breath and sometimes she just couldn't face being brave and cheerful any more.

'This is your opportunity,' another carer said to me, 'to prove how much you love your wife.'

Bloody hell, I thought. Soon someone will be telling me that this has all been 'a blessing in disguise'.

'Yes it is,' I wanted to say, 'but I'm not sure I'd describe it as an "opportunity".'

But I said 'thank you' in any case because she was right. It *was* a way of showing, and yes, *proving*, how much we loved her. This love was not about bold romantic declaration or saying the right thing at the right time, or about carefully chosen presents. Those days had gone, even though I did not acknowledge that yet. Now it was about the small things: the slow, patient and deliberate acts of care which we could not mess up because if we did then the consequences would be accident, pain and a quicker decline.

Danger, as the signs say at electricity substations. *Risk of Sudden Death*.

So, what *do* you say when a friend is terminally ill? One of the main things I have learned is that love is nothing if it is not practical. We are not judged by our intentions but our actions. *By your deeds thus shall ye know them*.

This was what Rosie and I were doing. We did not talk about how we were feeling or what it all meant because we were too busy problem-solving. At the same time, we tried to anticipate each stage of the illness, never quite knowing when the next descent was going to come, how steep the fall or how long it might last. Each time we got used to one stage we were on to the next. We were all instinct, all action. Everything was caught up in the moment of caring.

Our friends Florence and Richard came with beautifully constructed soups every other day: curried lentil, spicy tomato, Stilton and broccoli. Alex and Ruth brought sourdough and risotto, Jock and Charlotte arrived with Parmesan and bolognese and our neighbour Jane blended up a different energy juice or smoothie every day for five months. These were simple, everyday acts of kindness from 'the supporting cast' that we will never forget. Rosie and

I then had to add 'Tupperware wrangling' to our stage management of the daily theatre of illness. The front hall became our very own prop store, stacked up with piles of labelled tubs belonging to different people.

The actors kicked in with personalised audiobooks that were sent as attachments directly to Marilyn's phone. Pip Torrens recorded every single one of P. G. Wodehouse's tales of Jeeves and Bertie Wooster. Siobhán Redmond and Deborah Findlay read their favourite stories, Hetty Baynes took on Daphne du Maurier's *Rebecca*. Richard Williams found extracts from actors' diaries and told a wealth of anecdotes. His wife Joanna MacGregor played Chopin mazurkas. Gerda Stevenson sang a song and wrote Marilyn a poem. They were all doing what they were best at.

We received so many flowers that I had to ask people to stop. Our home was looking like a crematorium.

'I haven't died yet,' Marilyn said as I wheeled her back to the bedroom. 'Just in case you were wondering.'

My sister, Rebecca, made it as simple as possible. 'I'm going to send you flowers every Wednesday, the same size for the same vase. You just take the old ones out and put the new ones in. You must have *some* flowers.'

The friends who were not actors (or florists) posted scented candles and soaps and body milks and exotic shower gels. They were thoughtful gestures that helped us to make the most of being at home and made the rooms feel fresh and clean and light and aired. Philip Howard arrived at the same time as the district nurses and handed over a bottle of Givenchy's Dahlia Divin which certainly made a change from the morphine.

It was dangerous and upsetting and sentimental to send memories of holidays and happier times, but this, too, proved strangely comforting. Each week, Bill and Hildegard posted packages containing seven envelopes, a postcard memory or moment of beauty for each day: Matisse's *Two Models Resting*, Elfie Semotan's photograph of a man with a pigeon on his head in Venice, Vallotton's portrait of his wife ('It reminds us of you: Grace and Beauty') and Brancusi's *The Kiss*: 'It says Marilyn and James.'

Comedy was helpful. This wasn't the time for Chekhov, since we were in the middle of a Russian play of our own, but we watched black-and-white classics: all the Fred and Ginger movies, *Some Like It Hot*, *Bringing Up Baby*, *All About Eve*. Siobhán sent DVDs of films we didn't know so well starring Barbara Stanwyck and Rosalind Russell. In the afternoons Rosie nursed and tended Marilyn and they managed to get through the whole series of *Mad Men*, rationing themselves to two episodes at a time. And just as every day of 'lockdown with a terminal illness' was like a Sunday, in the evenings it was time for a period drama. We watched all the Jane Austen, Charles Dickens, George Eliot and Anthony Trollope adaptations we could find, playing our favourite game:

'When did they make this? Who's that actor again? Have you worked with him? Isn't he the one that was in, oh you know, that thing with— oh God, was it Penelope Wilton? Bill was in it too, wasn't he, or was that something else? Look, it's Pip when he had hair! There's Deborah – she should be in it more. God, the music's terrible. It's so badly lit! Derek Jacobi's wig is ridiculous. Wasn't Siobhán in this?'

Sometimes our emotions were hijacked by a plot twist or the death of a character that we hadn't been expecting. On other occasions we decided to confront the eye of the storm by watching the National Theatre relay of *A Monster Calls* in which a young boy has to learn how to come to terms with his mother's death from cancer. Then there was the Royal Ballet's production of *The Cellist*, about the life and death of Jacqueline du Pré. Watching this latter production, in which the magnificent dancer Lauren Cuthbertson moved from graceful ebullience to faltering and falling as multiple sclerosis took hold, was an act of hallucinatory madness. We could not believe that we were following all this; that we had *consciously* chosen to watch a ballet about a woman brought low, literally, by a muscle-wasting disease. I offered to turn it off but Marilyn said, 'No, let's keep going,' as if we were witnessing an illness become an art form. It was, perhaps, a way of framing what was going on, of converting it into theatre. This was another performance that we were going through, or a dream or a parallel life. God knows what it was. When it finished, we sat in silence, acknowledging that the dance had a strange redemptive grace. We had seen the imagined, idealised, balletic version of what life might be like for us in the next few weeks and months. Perhaps this could even be a way of thinking that it was beautiful?

When we ran out of things to say or it all got too much, we listened to music and watched concerts. I read a selection of new novels, some of which I had to put aside as they had too much suffering in them (Maggie O'Farrell's *Hamnet* was abandoned very early on even though we could tell it was a fine piece of writing because it was too good at describing illness). I then read my own just completed novel about Bach, out loud, which, like all my work, is about love and death and Marilyn.

When I approached the last chapter of the book, however, I couldn't continue. I found myself crying, unable to speak at all, and I remembered Dr R's words: *You have to survive it as best you can but in the end you just have to throw up your hands.*

Had we reached that stage? Marilyn smiled, and cried too, and I knew that reading the novel about Bach wasn't the most helpful thing to have done but we both wanted to do it if only because the publication was something to look forward to. It was something to share, another last production.

Charlotte read the whole of *The Hobbit*, *Three Men in a Boat* and *Mallory Towers*, one chapter at a time, and then *The Wind in the Willows*. After that she went on to the collected Wordsworth and any other poem Marilyn requested. She even read Christina Rossetti's poem by a daughter to her mother because, she said, it was loving and essential and had to be done.

To this day I just don't know how she managed to get through reading it out loud at all:

Sonnets are full of love, and this my tome
Has many sonnets: so here now shall be
One sonnet more, a love sonnet, from me
To her whose heart is my heart's quiet home,
To my first Love, my Mother, on whose knee
I learnt love-lore that is not troublesome;
Whose service is my special dignity,
And she my loadstar while I go and come.
And so because you love me, and because
I love you, Mother, I have woven a wreath
Of rhymes wherewith to crown your honoured name:
In you not fourscore years can dim the flame
Of love, whose blessed glow transcends the laws
Of time and change and mortal life and death.

Being Scottish

Marilyn was the second of three children born to an English mother and a Scots father. Her father built his own home in Markinch just after the Second World War, on the side of a hill overlooking the fields of Fife, the railway line and the Haig's whisky plant where he worked as an electrical engineer. His ancestors are all buried in the family plot in the cemetery close by. He was an amateur radio enthusiast, a keen golfer, and the treasurer of the local kirk; a fair-minded and tolerant Protestant without pretension who thought and expected the best of people. Marilyn inherited her sense of duty, justice and fair play from him, and her creativity, musicianship and daffiness from her mother, a Yorkshirewoman who had worked as a nurse in the war and was a splendid baker, singer and jazz pianist. The couple had both been married before. Her mother's first husband was an airman who had gone missing over France, and she had broken off with her family for dark and secret reasons that were never explained. Her father had been married and divorced but this was not discussed either. No one even knew the woman's name. The family mantra was that 'you should always tell the truth, but the truth need not always be spoken'; a belief that led to considerable trouble over the years.

I was born in Cambridge, but my father was a Liverpudlian Scot who fought in the Scots Guards and my branch of the Runcie family originates from Kilmarnock in Ayrshire. Throughout the nineteenth century our family had a draper's shop in the High Street selling suits, overcoats, workwear and even 'little-boy sailor suits for value *extraordinaire*'. I could, if I had the ability, play football or even rugby for Scotland, but my English public-school voice means that I can never pass myself off as a Scot: not even a posh one. I once read out the winning lottery numbers at half-time during a Raith Rovers game in Kirkcaldy but no one came forward because they could not understand what they called 'yer Cambridge accent'. I am a Scot by choice, an 'elected Scot', who still feels a bit of a fraud in the country; and yet I also feel enraged by some English assumptions about Scottish identity.

Two years after Marilyn and I married we moved south so that we could both continue to work for the BBC. I always felt guilty about taking her and Rosie away from their homeland. Neither of them could understand why the English liked imitating their accents as if this was something to be amused by, or how they thought Scots were tight-fisted, or why they refused to accept Scottish money when we were a supposedly 'United Kingdom'. Marilyn was infuriated when her English boss described one of her productions as 'remorselessly Scottish' and how so few people were able to see beyond the haggis, kilts and tartan, quoting P. G. Wodehouse's famous line 'it is never difficult to distinguish between a Scotsman with a grievance and a ray of sunshine.' In Paris, one friend offered Marilyn a glass of champagne assuming that she did not know what it was and had never had it before.

We lived in St Albans and commuted into London on crowded trains for twenty years until we finally couldn't stand it any more and went freelance and moved back to Edinburgh. During our exile, we would return to Scotland as often as we could, not least to see Marilyn's parents and get some proper fresh air. Then, we would drive on up from Fife to Skye and, as soon as we passed through either Glencoe or Crianlarich and saw the smooth roads narrow and the passing places begin, and the grandeur of the landscape open up in front of us, we felt a sense of expansive freedom. We played music very loudly, Big Country, Runrig's 'Once in a Lifetime', 'Letter from America', Barbara Dickson's 'Caravans' and my father's favourite:

Keep right on to the end of the road,
Keep right on to the end,
If the way be long, let your heart be strong,
Keep right on round the bend.

We rented the same house every year, just outside Elgol, with wonderful sunsets and a spectacular view of the Cuillins. It rained often, and there was a fierce wind, but we didn't care. There was always a view and books to read and walks to go on and wild flowers to collect and paint. We read Robert Louis Stevenson and Scottish poetry and the latest novels together with eccentricities such as *The Derk Isle*, a Tintin adventure translated into Scots. We delighted in the incongruity of a Belgian tale peppered with phrases like 'it's luikin dreich', 'dinna staund like a stookie', 'lat's sort oot this clanjamfrie' and 'Scunneration! It's Tintin.'

We found local fish and made soups and shortbread and took boat trips into Loch Coruisk, where Turner painted, and we bought whisky in the bay which Sorley MacLean described in his poem 'Shores':

If we were in Talisker on the shore
Where the great white foaming mouth of water
Opens between two jaws as hard as flint –
the Headland of Stones and the Red Point –
I'd stand forever by the waves
Renewing love out of their crumpling graves …

Dr Johnson came to Skye on his *Journey to Scotland and the Hebrides*, and on one of these holidays we developed the idea to make a play about his dictionary, his travels and his provocations about the country:

'What enemy would invade Scotland, where there is nothing to be got?'

'The noblest prospect which a Scotchman ever sees, is the high road that leads him to England!'

'Much may be made of a Scotchman – *if he be caught young.*'

And there is the famous dictionary definition of the word 'oats': 'a grain which in England is generally given to horses, but in Scotland supports the people'.

In the end, I wrote two plays, *A Word with Dr Johnson* and *Dr Johnson Goes to Scotland*, both performed at Òran Mór in Glasgow and the Traverse Theatre in Edinburgh. Marilyn directed them. They were, in effect, my love letter to Scotland and also a tribute to her, and a thank you for helping me to understand the country better and appreciate what it was like to live here.

Moving back was both a way of hoping for a better life and bringing Marilyn home after too long an exile. We were returning to our roots. In Fife, there was an Imrie who skippered a ship out of St Monans in the seventeenth century, there are Imries who still sail today, and there is a fish and chip shop in nearby Leven called Imries. A 'rouncie' is an old Scots word for horse, and a 'rouncieman' would be a 'keeper of horses'. (A 'runcie' is also old Scots for 'a crease or wrinkle' and 'a coarse woman of foul language, manners and appearance' but I'll let that go.)

Marilyn was so much happier whenever she was in Scotland. Her lungs seemed to open up, her shoulders broadened, her accent strengthened and she smiled and sang and laughed. She had so much more poise and ease and confidence away from the pressures of London. We loved the sea and the landscape and the mad everyday humour of a DIY store called Screw It, an Italian-owned chippy called The Codfather, and a gambling shop called Macbet. Marilyn was home again and came to be more carefree. Whenever she drove me through 'The Kingdom' and seemed to be going completely the wrong way, I would ask her if she was sure of the directions, and she would say, 'You can't go wrong in Fife. Every road takes you home in the end.' And I would reply, 'I suppose it just depends on how quickly you want to get there.' And she would smile and say, 'Are you not enjoying my company? Isn't this beautiful? Look at that view.'

I found it strange, having been brought up in the Oxfordshire countryside where I knew every road and lane, to find myself adapting to this increasingly familiar landscape; to become less English and more Scottish because of my marriage and heritage. I belonged and

I did not belong, but Marilyn was forging a new world for both of us.

It's not always easy. I was as tired as Nicola Sturgeon was after she had spoken at Holyrood and explained that Scotland was 'home to anyone who chooses to live here' only to be heckled with the remark 'except if you're English'. We don't need this kind of nonsense. But Scotland is as lovingly infuriating as any other nation. It can be both aggressive and nostalgic, angry and sentimental, and it sometimes has too fair a conceit of itself. The football is as erratic as the diet – and it must be the only country in the world where you can find a Michelin-starred restaurant next to a methadone clinic. Some people are so angry and drunk and out of it that they want nothing more than 'a square go'. To quote the playwright David Greig in his play *Dunsinane*, the only thing people *can* agree on is that it's cold. But the language and landscape of Scotland, its poetry and song, its enlightenment and its pioneering history, together with its humour and directness, still make it an imaginative and forthright place in which to live. A place of possibility. Marilyn's place. Our place. Home.

She Is Unable to Sing

One of the things I loved best about Marilyn was her voice, and the way she sang in the bathroom and as she walked through the house. It might have been an old folk song, a hymn, some Joni Mitchell or one of Strauss's *Last Songs*. It was a sign that she was happy, full of optimism, ready for whatever the day might bring. I remember saying to Charlotte, before her wedding day and in praise of her future husband, that the one thing I have learned is that it really helps if you marry a cheerful person.

Marilyn started out as a folk singer, playing the guitar and singing solos and duets with her sister in the pubs and clubs of Fife: 'Glasgow Peggy', 'Tarrytown', 'Four Marys', 'The Carls o' Dysart'. It was a way of earning money and having fun and she learned from established performers such as Ray and Archie Fisher, Cyril Tawney, Tom Paxton and the French Occitane singer Jacqueline Conte. She even appeared on television, a recording which is sadly lost, but there is an old reel-to-reel tape that Marilyn cleaned up and had converted into a CD so that it's possible to hear her sing as she did then, when she was nineteen:

Oh sister, sister, come tak a walk
Binnorie, o Binnorie,
And we'll hear the bonnie blackbird whistle ower his note
By the sweet mill dams o Binnorie.

When we began 'courting', that oddly traditional word that politely covers all manner of shenanigans, Marilyn sent me romantic songs about faithless lovers and distant soldiers and sailors, lost love and broken promises. She wrote them out quickly in letters and notes and scraps of paper because she knew them by heart. She used song as another way of talking, expressing her feelings, even saying what she could not say in words. 'Bushes and Briars' became a way of letting me know her fears:

Sometimes I am uneasy and troubled in my mind
Sometimes I think I'll go to my love and tell him my mind …

She knew that love always involves the dread of losing oneself, of falling so far you can't get back, that it carried such risk, but what was life without risk? We had to chance it all, and laugh and love the moment and so, at other times, she knew that she had to trust that love, or celebrate the fact that it could be absurd and ridiculous as well as fraught with danger and insecurity. She loved to be daft, to riff and to improvise, sending me a card playing on Elvis Presley's 'Are You Lonesome Tonight?':

R you lonesome tonight?
R you thinking of me now?
Rare hearts as one?
R the days when you're not here

Rduous – not fun?
R you lonesome tonight?

Or she crossed Bob Dylan's 'All I Really Want to Do' with a bit of Christopher Marlowe's 'Passionate Shepherd' so that the first letters spelled out my surname:

Really all I want to do, is be
Undressed alone with you
Now I know it's you I love
Come let us all pleasures prove
In bed or out, you're my sweetheart
Every day's a year when we're apart.

When I came back from filming in America, and she was at work, Marilyn left instructions for me to play Joni Mitchell's 'A Case of You'.

'Lined up in the CD player, sweetcakes!'

And I sat on the bed and fell asleep to Joni singing about being in my blood like holy wine and thinking yes, that love was even more than touching souls, it was about being so completely intertwined that you couldn't work out whether any part of you was separate any more; that she had made me whatever I was and would continue to define me and that I could not be described without her.

Marilyn taught a song-writing course at Dartington with her friend Sally Davies where she would draw examples from traditional folk songs such as 'Tom of Bedlam', 'The Outlandish Knight' and 'The Twa' Sisters', and then move on to 'Papa Was a Rollin' Stone' by the Temptations and Joni Mitchell's 'The Last Time I Saw Richard'. Together, we loved to look out for contemporary examples of song as a form of compressed storytelling, whether it was in Eminem's 'Stan', 'A Grand Don't Come for Free' by the Streets or Plan B's 'The Defamation of Strickland Banks'.

She often began her creative-writing classes with 'The Dying Soldier':

When I was on horseback wasn't I pretty?
When I was on horseback wasn't I gay?
O wasn't I pretty when I entered Cork City
When I met with my downfall on the fourteenth of May?

Straight away, you have the place, the date, and the exact moment when the story turns, all in the first verse. Songs show you how to include only what is necessary, and her editing of my novels stressed the need for focus and rhythm and the elimination of excess. Sometimes this meant losing the sections of which I was most proud.

'Do we really need this character?' she would write in the margin, or 'You've done this' or 'Cut!', or an even more brutal 'No! No! No!'

One of her favourite productions was *Dusty Won't Play*, Annie Caulfield's account of Dusty Springfield's tour of apartheid South Africa in 1964 when she refused to perform to segregated audiences. She worked with the singer Frances Thorburn, a blisteringly brilliant actor. It was a show with such bravura and attack, all high-wire, all Frances and all Marilyn, the pleasure of giving it out to a crowd: 'Don't worry, we know how to do this. You're in good hands. Just enjoy it. Just be thrilled.' As soon as it began you could hear the intake of breath from the audience: 'My God, that is Dusty.'

It was a long time after her death before I could listen to the CD of Marilyn singing, hearing the love and joy in her performance, recognising the delight she took in the sheer act of letting her voice run free. I remembered telling people, 'She only sings when she is happy,' and the desperate end of the diagnosis: 'She is unable to sing.'

I waited until she was asleep and listened to her breathing, thinking of 'Every Breath You Take' by the Police and trying to forget that it is actually a song about stalking. Difficulty breathing is a symptom of MND. By a couple of months into the diagnosis, I had become used to the new, terrifying gaps in her erratic breathing, the long pauses when she didn't seem to be breathing at all. I didn't know if her death was going to be tonight or tomorrow night or this week or in a few months. I tried to breathe to the same rhythm so that we could calm each other down. I tried to imagine I WAS her, and what it would be like if I was dying instead of her.

I thought of her carrying voice, her breath control, songs in the shower and as she came out of the bathroom and back into the bedroom:

> As I walked out one morning in the springtime of the year
> I overheard a young sailor or likewise his lady fair
> They sang a song together made the valleys for to ring
> While the birds on the spray in the meadow gay
> Proclaimed the lovely spring.

Sometimes she would continue drying herself and shake out the talcum powder and sing directly and only to me:

> Said the sailor to his sweetheart, we soon must sail away
> But it's lovely on the water to hear the music play
> But if I had my way, my dearest love,
> Along with you I'd stay.

On my desk is the last Valentine card she gave me. It's a red heart placed on a score of music. The heart is outlined by gold wire holding a pearl at its centre. Inside she has written: 'You make my heart sing.'

The One Light We Keep On

Mrs Patrick Campbell observed that 'wedlock is the deep, deep peace of the double bed after the hurly-burly of the chaise longue.' On one holiday in Paris, we went to the Musée d'Orsay and saw Toulouse-Lautrec's famous painting of *The Bed* and Marilyn said, 'Look, it's us, except they're the wrong way round.'

The last Christmas present she gave me was a quilted coverlet for the enormous double bed she had bought for my birthday the previous year. Until then, we had slept in the big brass bed she had kept from her first marriage, and I tried not to mind about this because people tend to hang on to the furniture. I thought of my friend Tom's mother who died in the same bed that she was born in.

But it wasn't long before this new bed and its coverlet had to be moved so the hospital bed could come in. We slept side by side but not in the same bed, neither of us ever saying and both of us knowing that this was the room in which Marilyn was going to die.

We had always found it easy to talk at night. Marilyn called it 'the best part of the day'. It was a way of shutting out the world and being with each other. Now we had to be more careful, time was limited and she was losing the power of speech altogether. Soon there would be no more conversation at all, or I would be talking to her in my head and imagining her replies rather than hearing them directly.

One night, when she could still speak and wanted to share everything, she checked that I was still awake and then said to me in the darkness: 'I don't mind if you marry again, you know.'

And so, just before sleep, I found myself in the middle of a play without a script. I had to be so careful what to say, not just because whatever I said might be wrong, but because she found it hard to speak physically and she must have been gearing up for this, trying to find the right time, wanting the subject aired.

'You do,' I said.

'No, I don't. And I know you will.'

Pause.

'I haven't thought about that at all.'

'Have you imagined it?'

'No, it's ridiculous to think about that now.'

'I know you have.'

This was impossible. I had, of course I had, before I had any knowledge that she was *dying*. Because before then I think, like many middle-aged people (at least I hope I'm right), I had thought about what it might be like to have been married to X instead, if circumstances had been different or life had changed, or if I had never met Marilyn in the first place.

People look back to former loves and mad infatuations and make all kinds of delusional imaginative projections and most of the time they are absurd fantasies. You indulge them to the point of ridiculousness. You even manage to bore yourself. Then you pull yourself together and get on with your life as you should have been doing all along.

But now that Marilyn was still beside me (for how long?) in the dark, and we were together and close and more intimate and fragile and frightened than we had ever been, it was inconceivable to think of being with anyone else, or for anything ever to matter more than this conversation with this person who was so much a part of me lying beside me. *Inconceivable.*

'As long as you're buried with me,' she said.

This was easy to answer.

'I will be.'

'I don't want to be cremated. You know we talked about having our ashes scattered in Venice? I don't want that any more.'

'St Monans?'

'Yes.'

'Burial. I understand.'

Pause – in which I thought, This is too terrible, too mad, I have to think of something to change the mood, to stop her getting too depressed and introverted – although why should she not?

'I could still go first,' I said.

'Don't joke.'

'I will always love you. You know that. You will always be the love of my life.'

'You don't know that.'

Pause.

'I'd have to live to ninety-eight to be with someone longer than you.'

Pause.

'You've worked it out already?'

'I just did it in my head. I wasn't *thinking about it.*'

'I bet you were.'

'I wasn't.' *Pause*. 'You know I love you best. That this is best.'

'I know. I love you best too.'

Pause – in which neither of us knew what to say and I was just about to say 'Night night' again, thinking that all this was finished and she should stop being anxious but why should she not be, she was dying for God's sake, when Marilyn said, 'I think I'd rather you just had a string of affairs with women who can't possibly live up to me.'

This was impossible to predict or answer and it was not helpful to go any further down this route. 'I'll do my best, then,' I said.

'I'm sure you will.'

'None of them will ever come close. You do know that?'

'You say that now.'

'I mean that now.'

This was too raw. But how much time did we have left when she could articulate any of this?

'Let's not argue,' I said. 'You don't have to worry.'

(And I knew that was the wrong thing to say even then but how could I get through one of the last proper conversations we were ever going to have without saying the wrong thing at least once? Never had both of us been so careful of conversation.)

'No, I won't. But I hope I'll be watching over you.'

'You don't need to hope ...'

'Like the song ...'

'"Someone to watch over me". I'll imagine you watching anyway. You know you'll always be with me.'

'I hope that's true.'

'I know it's true.'

Pause.

Was this the end of the conversation? Could we go to sleep now?

'Night night,' she said. 'And thank you.'

'I love you.'

'I love YOU.'

And I leant over and kissed her on the lips and we both knew her body was failing and I wanted to say to her: 'If I ever love anyone again then *part* of what they love in me, or even *most* of what they love in me, will be *you*.'

But I couldn't say this because I could already hear her saying, 'Well, that is of no comfort to me,' or even her usual response when she knew that I was winning an argument but could not accept it.

'That's true.'

It used to infuriate me. 'That's true? Why can't you just admit that I am right?'

But then we were hopeless at arguments. Every time she was cross with me, I felt so terrible that I was sure my insides were emptying and I wanted to go to the bathroom. This happened so often that she used to shout just as she was getting to her main point: 'Don't wriggle out of it now by pissing off to the lavatory!'

And then there was the time I couldn't stop pressing home my point, I can't remember what it was about, and she said to me, 'Oh, just fuck off and grow up, James Runcie.'

And I said, 'What do you want me to do first? Fuck off and then grow up or grow up and then fuck off?'

She was furious with my pettiness, and I was reminded of being a precocious thirteen-year-old boy, a git really, at my prep school, and the housemaster continually warning us not to talk after lights out and then finally snapping and coming in and turning on all the lights and shouting to a room full of twelve prepubescent boys: 'WHO IS TALKING? WHO IS TALKING?'

And I replied, 'You are, sir,' and got hit with six of the best with a slipper for the cheek of it all.

It was absurd to think of all this now, life in a school dormitory, and I realised that Marilyn's hospital bed was equally so institutional, so resolutely, so practically, so defensively single.

At the Frieze Art Fair in 2018, the Ingleby Gallery showed a group of paintings by Andrew Cranston. They were the size of the spine and cover of a hardback book, unframed and applied directly to the wall, and they were arresting in their eerie directness: a girl and a dog, four heads bobbing in the sea, a baby crawling across a carpet, a semi-nude woman ironing with the steam rising in front of her breasts like a modern Bonnard. They had extraordinary titles: *Loyalty to a Nightmare*, *It Seems So Long Ago*, *In Solace of Dogs*, *If I Were a Carpenter*.

I was particularly drawn to a painting of a couple in bed, because it seemed like a variant on the Toulouse-Lautrec painting Marilyn and I had stood before in Paris. This was all white duvet for two-thirds of the picture, and only the heads of the couple were visible. But they looked like us when we were younger, and again they were the wrong way round. It was called *The Innocents* and I was determined to buy it on a whim. Us in bed. We could hang it in the bedroom. It would be lovely.

'What about this instead?' said Marilyn, standing over to the left and looking at something completely different. 'I think it's more evocative. More mysterious. You have to think about the story behind it.'

It was a dark painting, khaki and sombre green, of a room with a table and three chairs lit by a single Victorian lamp. Painted in enamel oil on the cover of a hardback book by Victor Hugo, it was called *The One Light We Keep On*. It was the artwork the gallery used to advertise the show. They had only just put it up.

'Let's buy it,' I said. Only later did we read the artist's note about it: 'The light maybe of a writer, a night writer. Maybe W. S. Graham, the night-fisherman catching his poems in his nets … The hour is very late or very early or, as my friend Eddie Summerton calls it, "between the late and early". Four in the morning. The hour of the wolf. The hour that most people die and most babies are born.'

It is the time I always wake up, when I wonder if I am still dreaming or not. The painting now hangs in the hall, and every time I pass it to go in or out of the house, I think of that day with Marilyn in the autumn of 2018 before we knew that anything was wrong, and I remember the Smiths song 'There Is a Light That Never Goes Out' and I know beyond all doubt and with all my certainty that her light will be the light that I always keep on.

Goodbye, Old Life!

From: *The Cherry Orchard*.

LUBOV: Let's go!
LOPAKHIN: Are you all here? There's nobody else? There's a lot of things in there. I should lock everything up. Come on!
ANYA: Goodbye, old house! Goodbye, old life!
TROFIMOV: Welcome, new life.
LOPAKHIN: Until the spring, then! Come on … till we meet again! [*Exit.*]

There are moments of grim humour amidst the dying. 'I am not in pain,' Marilyn told me (although this was not true), 'and I have not lost my mind. At least I have been spared cancer and dementia. I'll leave that to you.'

The nutritionist telephoned to discuss the inevitability of a liquid-only diet and the need for proper vitamins. There were some new flavours of Complan that she thought Marilyn might like.

'I would rather die than eat Complan,' Marilyn replied. 'In fact, I *will* die rather than eat Complan.'

I wrote friends a long and desperate email, letting them know that the end would not be far away. *To imagine it in Chekhovian terms, it's a little like the end of* The Cherry Orchard — *imagine a lit house on a summer evening with no one in it but an elderly servant going round and slowly blowing out all the candles one by one until the darkness comes.*

When Marilyn demanded I show it to her, she was furious, particularly about the reference to Chekhov.

'It's so self-indulgent.'

'But it's the truth. We can't put on a show any more. We have to tell people what's going on.'

Marilyn did not want her friends to know any of the grim and humiliating reality. She hoped that everything would continue to be as right as it possibly could be — even when it wasn't. Although she was a 'patient' patient, she couldn't accept or come to terms with what was happening. She never wanted to die. I couldn't ever persuade her to make her peace or reach a state of resignation and I think that I will always feel a failure for not inspiring any readiness in her. She hated the fact that she was dying until the end.

I once gave a lecture in the National Library of Scotland about David Hume and the exact moment that he realised he was going to die. He was composing a short, handwritten autobiography, twelve and a quarter pages in length, entitled 'My Own Life'. It is dated 18 April 1776 — two months after he had bought his own grave plot for £4, and four months before his death.

At first glance it is not a particularly exciting read; a personal entry, perhaps, for the *Dictionary of National Biography*. But then something extraordinary happens; for this document contains what I believe to be the most telling grammatical change in the history of literature.

After recounting the story of his literary career, his employment in France and his return to Edinburgh, Hume announces the onset of his final illness. 'In spring 1775 I was struck with a disorder in my bowels which at first gave me no alarm, but has since, as I apprehend it, become mortal and incurable. I now reckon on a speedy dissolution.'

The words are specific – mortal, incurable, a dissolution.

This was happening to Hume as he wrote; and yet he was also sanguine: 'I possess the same ardour as ever in study, and the same gaiety in company. I consider besides, that a man of sixty-five, by dying, cuts off only a few years of infirmities; and – though I see many symptoms of my literary reputation's breaking out at last with additional lustre – I know that I had but a few years to enjoy it. It is difficult to be more detached from life than I am at present.'

He had reached a state of acceptance and was ready for death.

Now comes the crucial switch. It occurs right in the middle of the sentence: 'To conclude historically with my own character – I am, or rather *was* (for that is the style I must now use in speaking of myself; which enables me the more to speak my sentiments), I was, I say, a man of mild dispositions, of command of temper, of an open social, and cheerful humour, capable of attachment, but little susceptible of enmity, and of great moderation in all my passions.'

This is one of the great statements of the Enlightenment. David Hume realised the enormity of what he was saying *as he was writing it down*; the fact, and the impact of his death, suddenly hit him – his pen in his hand – and he moved from the present to the past, and from life to death, in the same sentence.

'I am …' he began, and you can sense him stopping. You can almost see the pen in the air above the paper.

You can hear, in that slightest of pauses, Hume correcting himself: '… or rather *was*'.

In my experience authors often do not know what they really think until they write it down. They discover their thoughts in the process of writing. It is the act of writing itself that articulates both thought and emotion.

So in reading this passage you can hear David Hume thinking aloud; and stopping.

Now he must collect himself. He returns the pen to the paper and picks up the pace of the prose with an explanation and a justification ('for that is the style I must now use in speaking of myself; which enables me the more to speak my sentiments').

He realises that this switch of tense makes him free. He does not need to worry about what people will think. When people read this, he will be dead. He can say what he likes; the idea of death liberates his prose.

There then follows a list of his achievements. But these are not *literary* achievements – they are achievements of *character*. He was, he says, 'a man of mild dispositions, of command of temper, of an open social, and cheerful humour, capable of attachment, but little susceptible of enmity, and of great moderation in all my passions … even my love of literary fame, my ruling passion, never soured my humour, notwithstanding my frequent disappointments …'

Cheerfulness, warmth of character and good company are of equivalent, or of even greater benefit, to reputation than literary achievement. 'Mr Hume,' his cousin, the

Reverend John Home, wrote, 'in the latter part of his life, retired to his native country, and devoted the evening of his days to Hospitality, Elegance, Literature and Friendship.'

These were our values. It's what Marilyn and I believed in. Hospitality, Elegance, Literature and Friendship. Now I thought it was my duty to help her come to terms with what was happening and approach the end with the sagacity of David Hume.

Except she wasn't David Hume. She was Marilyn, and she hated everything that was happening. I couldn't foist my opinions and expectations upon her or help her to come to terms with what was happening at all. She had to find her own way of dying, and this was private, almost secret. I never really knew how much she was protecting me from her pain and her feelings or what she thought and feared in her darkest moments because, of course, she could hardly speak. She would listen, and nod, and give little instructions when she could, but she was beginning to be locked in to the intense and devastating loneliness of dying.

We would just have to talk to each other as much as we could and while she was still able to do so. After that, we would have to rely on our mutual love and understanding. The unspoken love. The understood love.

This is now the hardest bit to write.

Because there was no way to predict when the end might come, I said goodbye to her four times. The first two were frightened brevities, 'just in case' farewells, making sure that she knew I loved and would always love her. The third was more urgent, when she could hardly speak at all and I really thought that she might die *that very night*. I hadn't prepared anything. I wasn't David Hume. You don't ever quite think of the last words you might want to say to your beloved, you just have to say them, even if they come out wonky.

So I began to talk to Marilyn as she lay beside me, breathing erratically. I told her that it was all right, I would look after the girls, and we would look after each other, and she had given us so much love that it would sustain all our futures. We would never be without her. Then, just as I was hitting full flight, telling her that I had always loved and adored her and how she would always be a part of me, and that it was impossible to think of myself as a separate person, she said, very quietly: 'Enough.'

I didn't know whether this was editing or because she had got the message or because she couldn't say anything in return. I think it was probably that she couldn't bear to hear all this and to think about what we were both losing. Perhaps it was also to spare me getting upset, even though I had tried not to cry. I wanted to be clear and consoling and full of steadfast love.

I Corinthians 15:58. *Be ye steadfast, immovable, always abounding in the work of the Lord, knowing that your toil in the Lord is not in vain.*

I once staged a non-stop reading of the King James Bible at the Bath Literature Festival. It took ninety-six hours and thirty-eight minutes. I was interviewed about it on Radio 4 and Marilyn recorded the interview on her phone and kept it there because, she said, 'I guessed what they were going to ask and I knew what you were going to say.'

The presenter wondered about my favourite verse and I told him it was from the Book of Ruth and he asked me to read it: *And Ruth said, 'Entreat me not to leave thee, or to return from following after thee: for whither thou goest, I will go; and where thou lodgest, I will lodge: thy people shall be my people, and thy God my God. Where thou diest, will I die, and there will I be buried: the LORD do so to me, and more also, if ought but death part thee and me.'*

But now Marilyn really was leaving me and I tried to tell her that it was all right to let go. She didn't have to keep on fighting. I was 'entreating' her to leave and I had to say this without sounding as if I *wanted* her to die.

I just couldn't believe her suffering, *I could not stand it.* Her breathing became steady and yet desperate. I couldn't take in that she had four or five days of fight still left in her, even when she could no longer eat or drink. But on the last evening I knew that we were approaching the end. We all did, because the carers left in tears.

The girls performed their nightly ritual of rubbing her favourite lavender-scented cream into her sore arms, and Charlotte read her Wordsworth's 'Daffodils'. They lit a candle and kissed her goodnight.

Then Marilyn and I were alone. I had said goodbye three times already and been told that it was 'enough'. What to do? Should I repeat myself? I had said all that I had to say. There were no more words.

But there was music. We listened to the whole of Purcell's *Dido and Aeneas* with the great aria 'When I Am Laid in Earth'. I discovered the recording of Teresa Stich-Randall singing Schubert's 'Ave Maria' that we had listened to together on vinyl just after we had found each other. We were remembering the love we had when we first met and the world was all before us.

In my end is my beginning.

I found Andreas Scholl singing 'Che Faro' from Gluck's *Orfeo*, that great desperate lament as Orpheus sings of his love for Eurydice, and how he cannot bear to live without her, and he looks back to see her because he cannot think

89

of doing anything else, and I promised Marilyn that I would always turn back, I would never not see her, she would always be with me, wherever I was, wherever she was.

I fell asleep. We all did. We couldn't stay awake any longer.

And then, in the darkest hours of the night, as Marilyn slept beside me, with the whole house quiet and at peace, her ragged breathing stopped, and she died.

Son of a Preacher Man

Like doctors, many children of the clergy enter the same profession as their parents; or they go off the rails, reacting violently to the idea of sacrifice and goodness. But I think they also inherit a desire to be heard and to entertain, and so it's no surprise that showbusiness is a strange by-product of a religious upbringing: Laurence Olivier, Alice Cooper, Denzel Washington, David Tennant and Katy Perry are all children of clerics. There is a theatricality to the pulpit, procession and common worship.

I was brought up in the village of Cuddesdon, in the Oxfordshire countryside, where the rituals of birth, marriage and death were marked every day. It was a world where tragedy came to the house. I remember being six years old and answering the door when my father was out. I had to remember a message. 'Kevin Dymock has been knocked off his motorbike. He has internal bleeding. He may not last the night.'

And yet it was also comic. My father's secretary, Mrs Maguire, said that when her husband left her for another woman, it was the mistress who came back to fetch his things. 'What does he like for his tea?' she asked, and the devout Mrs Maguire told my father, 'I was so angry, Vicar, this great red mist descended upon me, and I thought of the rudest thing I could say to her and I just spat it out. *Harpic*, I said.'

Mrs Maguire is the name of the housekeeper in my detective series, *The Grantchester Mysteries*, and the central character, Sidney Chambers, is a tribute both to the maverick eighteenth-century clergyman Sydney Smith and to my father. He is also, naturally, a clerical version of me, imagining a different life I might have led, and Hildegard, his German wife, self-indulgently named after my friend Hildegard Bechtler, is very much Marilyn in disguise.

When I told my father that I wanted to marry her he looked very dubious. My parents had only met her once. Afterwards my mother had said, 'She's very nice but it'll never last.'

'Are you asking for my advice or are you telling me?' my father asked. We were sitting in his study in the middle of Lambeth Palace. There are less intimidating places.

'I'm telling you.'

'Well, then. We'll do everything we can to support you.'

He couldn't marry us in church because Marilyn was a divorcee, but he could still bless us, and rather than reminding us of Dr Johnson's dictum that a second marriage is 'the triumph of hope over experience' he gave us a leather-bound Bible and wrote in the front in big bold handwriting: 'LOVE NEVER FAILS.' He even underlined it.

It was only a few years after he had married Prince Charles and Princess Diana, with the oft-quoted phrase, 'Here is the stuff of which fairy tales are made: the Prince and Princess on their wedding day.' But whenever it is referenced, people fail to remember the warning that follows: 'But fairy tales usually end at this point with the simple phrase, "They lived happily ever after." This may be because fairy stories regard marriage as an anticlimax after the romance of courtship. This is not the Christian view. Our faith sees the wedding day not as the place of arrival but the place where the adventure really begins ...'

Marilyn and I married in a registry office in Dunbar, in East Lothian, looking out to sea. The service of blessing was held three days later in Lambeth Palace Chapel with music by Thomas Tallis and William Walton and Harvey and the Wallbangers, with seven-year-old Rosie as the flower girl. It was celebratory and sombre, and my father was determined that we obeyed all the rules and said the prayer of penitence out loud and in front of everyone.

We offer and present to you, Lord, ourselves, our souls and bodies, our thoughts and deeds, our desires and prayers. Forgive what we have been, consecrate what we are, and direct what we shall be, in your mercy and in your love.

He may have been considered 'a wet' by the press at the time, but he was nothing like that when it came to matters of faith:

Let their love for each other be a seal upon their hearts, a mantle about their shoulders, and a crown upon their foreheads. Bless them in their work and in their companionship; in their sleeping and in their waking; in their joys and in their sorrows; in their life and in their death.

I could still preach some of his marriage sermons to this day. He told each congregation that the best present they could give each happy couple was not a food mixer or a set of table napkins but that 'as they pledge themselves to each other before the altar of God, they are surrounded and supported by the sincere affection and genuine prayer of family and friends. That is a present for a lifetime.'

The celebrant then addresses the congregation, saying: 'Will ye who have witnessed these promises do all in your power to uphold these two persons in their marriage?'

People: 'We will.'

Marilyn and I were not regular churchgoers, nor did we pray regularly even though she sometimes wished that we would. I had always been somewhat distrustful of the phrase 'the family that prays together stays together' and, having had an evangelical Christian girlfriend in the past, I am dubious about public demonstrations of belief, preferring to keep my fluctuating attitude to Christianity private.

But I cannot avoid writing about faith, love and death. They are my only subjects, even if I cannot fully trust in the promise that an all-powerful God has an actively benevolent presence in the world. Perhaps I have always been guilty of taking Pascal's wager that it is more prudent to believe than not. It's an insurance policy for eternity. Therefore, whenever I have been asked about it publicly, I have tended to hide behind Thomas Carlyle's idea of a life of doubt enriched by faith.

I came unstuck twice when promoting the prequel to *The Grantchester Mysteries*: once at the Barnes Literary Festival where a woman asked me if I believed, was unsatisfied by my reply and asked, 'Well, do you go to church? Do you pray? You can't be half-hearted about this' – and then again, when I was interviewed for the Salvation Army magazine, *War Cry*. I was expecting the usual cosy little interview, but it began with this question: 'How would you describe your relationship with Jesus?'

'A bit on and off,' I replied, which was hardly satisfactory. I seem to want to have it both ways. I like to be part of the club when I do go to church and can be positively hypocritical with people who take up the option of Christianity *lite*.

I am stroppy, for example, with people in England who pretend to be Christian in order to get their children into a good free Church of England or Catholic school – how they're all eager to help film the nativity play or edit the school magazine but as soon as their kids have got their A levels they're never seen in church again. *Bye!*

And I am unfairly judgemental when people who are, at best, agnostics use historic churches as some kind of drop-in centre for baptisms, weddings and funerals to give their relentlessly secular lives an Instagram-friendly spiritual pit stop.

So, I have sympathy with a vicar at a recent wedding who called a halt to the first hymn when no one was singing it properly. 'Stop, stop, stop – I know you're only here for the architecture – but *make an effort*.'

And there comes a time when you really do have to make up your mind about your faith; and that time is probably when one of you is faced with a terminal illness.

We were sitting looking out to sea in St Monans and I asked Marilyn if she wanted to talk about faith and the funeral and what she thought about God.

'Oh, I'm still quite keen on him,' she said, 'in spite of what he's done to me.'

I had tried to prepare for this moment in my writing. Sidney's wife dies at the end of *The Grantchester Mysteries* and I wrote it in a wild haze of anticipatory grief, long before any diagnosis, just to protect myself, and it had gone down very badly with the rest of the family. ('I hope you're not expecting praise,' said Charlotte.)

But no matter how much you try to imagine what you might feel, to anticipate a situation is by no means to understand it. Everything still comes as a shock and I'm not at all sure if you ever quite get to the stage when 'the readiness is all' or steady yourself for how you are going to feel when you find yourself sitting next to your wife on the bench of desolation.

I asked Marilyn if she'd like to see our friend Neil Gardner, the minister at Canongate Kirk, whom she had mentioned in her plans for the memorial service.

'I would. If he can come. Not on the phone.'

At the peak of Covid the only help being offered was online and on the telephone; but Neil came to the house and kept his social distance and we talked quite naturally and easily about the funeral service as if we were preparing for some kind of party.

We discussed what might be possible under lockdown, not knowing when on earth this was all going to take place, but we had decided on a burial, not a cremation, in St Monans, on the headland looking out to the Firth of Forth. There would be a piper and psalms of the sea. Neil understood. He'd done this before. He is, as we like to say in our family, 'a proper priest', serious and compassionate, kind and funny. He believes that there is a future for our deepest loves and, as he spoke and prayed, I felt the reassurance of centuries of faith.

O Lord, support us all the day long of this troublous life, until the shades lengthen, and the evening comes, and the busy

world is hushed, the fever of life is over, and our work is done.
Then Lord in your mercy grant us safe lodging, a holy rest and
peace at the last; through Jesus Christ our Lord. Amen.

After Marilyn's death, the consolations of Christianity
arrived from the most surprising places. Heather, a friend
in St Monans, sent me a simple text: *Psalm 34 v 18 God is*
close to the broken-hearted.

Our feisty no-nonsense dry-cleaners handed me
this card:

Dear Mr Runcie and family
We are so sorry for your loss.
May God's grace enable you to see a future laced with hope,
and may you be given the gift of faith to trust HIM in all
things. As one day gives way to another, so may darkness gives
way to light, sadness yield to joy, and despair surrender to hope
in you.
Thinking of you all at this sad time
Michelle and Marcia

When Marilyn had first taken me to St Monans in 1987,
to see Scotland's closest church to the sea, the one with
the boat hanging from the centre of the nave, we arrived
in the middle of a funeral. It seemed to involve all the men
and women in the village, the sexes separated and dressed
in black. The only sounds were of a tolling bell, footsteps
on gravel, the cawing of the rooks and a distant sea. It
was cold and sombre, respectful and strangely unforgiving.
This is what we do here, the village seemed to be saying, *and*
this is what we have always done. We keep the faith.

We moved to the village in 2016, anticipating many
years together and a long and happy retirement, and, after

we had made some initial adjustments, we decided to re-do the kitchen, asking Alan, the local joiner, if he could organise the refit. He came round, a calm, wise man, who looked like Father Christmas. As is traditional in a Scottish village, he was also the undertaker, and an elder in the kirk, and he was the man you needed to get onside if you were to be a part of the community.

Marilyn quickly made it clear that she had been born in Fife, that she knew the area well, her father worked at Haig's and she had gone to nearby Buckhaven High. Alan immediately started speaking to her as if he had known her all his life.

When I had to tell him that she was terminally ill, he couldn't quite believe what I was saying. There were long pauses. I didn't know if he could still hear me or if the line had gone dead. I told him I was worried that we were in Edinburgh, he was in Fife and we were in the middle of a pandemic. There was a silence and then he said with infinite kindness, as if he were my father or even my grandfather, 'Don't you worry about any of this. Leave it with me. Call when the time comes and we'll be there. You have only one thing to do. Look after her. She's a fine woman.'

After Marilyn died, Alan came within an hour and a half with his son and one other undertaker. He stood at the foot of the bed, and lowered his head, half bowing, as in prayer, acknowledging her death. Then he told me to wait with the girls in another room. We should leave it to him. And then they carried my wife out of the house forever.

We travelled on behind as soon as we were ready. We could not bear to think of Marilyn in St Monans without us. Alan stopped at the house and assured us that all was well, she was in the Chapel of Rest, and he'd give her the funeral he'd hope for himself. I told him that I wanted it to be as traditional as possible, in accordance with all the rites of the Church of Scotland. We decided on a simple oak coffin with rope handles, the kind a sailor might have, with garlands of flowers from the fields and farms of Fife.

The funeral was on 1 September 2020. There were eleven of us when there should have been hundreds. But these were still the days of Covid. Alan arrived and shook my hand and Neil sat with the hearse. It was ten forty-five in the morning, on a bright and clear day. The tide was on the way out, which seemed appropriate. We sat in the cars, and Alan walked ahead of us all with his frock coat and velvet top hat and walking stick – I didn't know it was called *paging* until then – and people in the village stood outside their doors to watch us pass as we travelled through the harbour and up the hill to the kirk and cemetery.

It all took place in the open air and the piper walked us in to 'MacCrimmon's Lament'. Neil stood beside the grave and read from the psalms and prayed. He talked of Marilyn's love of the sea and Christ calming the storm and how the storm of her life had passed and now she could rest. She had no need of her body any more. The coffin was lowered and we threw rose petals and held on to each other, and I couldn't believe that we were doing this now, in a beautiful village, and that this life-force, wife, mother, sister, friend, was no longer with us. Surely this was all a dream, my whole life was a dream, this could not be right, but this calm man was speaking, and it was a magnificent day in an extraordinary place, and it felt as right as it could possibly be. It was everything she had asked for, and we had done it, even though I had never really imagined doing any such thing at all.

The piper played 'The Flooers o' the Forest', and then we were not sure what to do next. He started to lead us away, back home, and we were leaving Marilyn there in the graveyard without us and it seemed so wrong to abandon her. I looked out to sea and remembered my mother and father and their deaths too, and the loss of Marilyn, my greatest love who could never be replaced. Then I thought of the words from the Song of Solomon: *Many waters cannot quench love. Neither can the floods drown it.*

There were gulls swooping low over the far-off water and the light was sharp on the horizon. The day was reaching out for completion: life continuing without her.

After …

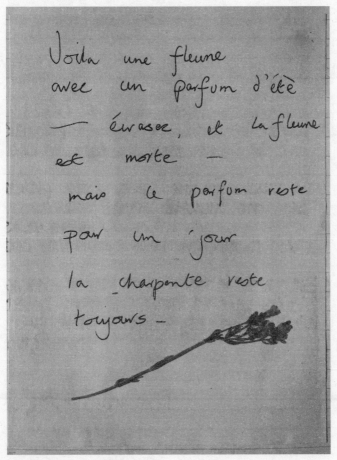

Marilyn's notebook, France

Solo

I had never lived on my own before. Everything became strange and dream-like, as if I was inhabiting someone else's life. I couldn't quite believe how any of this had happened. There didn't seem to be any *point* to anything I was doing. I found a card Marilyn had given me, a cut-out of a ship's anchor in blue and white. On the back she had written: 'You are my soul's anchor.' Well, now I was anchorless.

Was this the beginning of old age, I wondered, in which the days feel so long and yet the years are so short?

When we first moved to St Monans, Marilyn was sixty-eight years old and told our friend Hildegard that she was hoping 'for ten good years here'. In the end, we had three and a bit.

My two-year-old granddaughter looked at a picture of Marilyn taken in a garden when she was forty and smiling and had so much life ahead of her: 'Do you want her to come back?'

I said I did.

'But she can't,' Bea told me. 'She died.'

'I know,' I said. 'It's very sad.'

She put her hand to her chest as her mother had taught her and said, 'Grandma in our hearts.'

I read her stories to stop myself crying. I even made one up, about a man who lived his whole life upside down. Then it was time for Bea to go home and I was on my own once more. What to cook and what to remember? What does a widower do with the seemingly endless days ahead?

Time stretched away because there was no urgency. Friends told me that I could do anything I liked. But what did I like? How was I to live now, not so much in the shadow of death but in the darkness of grief?

Sometimes, it was the stupid little things (setting out two cups for coffee in the morning and then realising that I only needed one), receiving her post (Sun Life Assurance guaranteeing a lump sum of £10,000 – *I don't think so*), or remembering that Marilyn always used to accuse me of never putting back the bathmat – *well, I'm certainly putting it back now*. These everyday details were intermingled with the enormous things (not hearing her voice, not having anyone to tell me that they loved me, sleeping alone, imagining her breathing as if she were still alive and beside me in the night).

In the past, whenever anything went wrong in life or at work (an argument with a friend, an impossible television presenter, a bitchy review of one of my books) I would return to her as my strength and shield. *You can say what you like, I don't care, because I've got my wife.*

Marilyn once directed J. M. Barrie's play, *What Every Woman Knows*. First performed in 1908, it's about the feckless son of an aristocrat who only survives as an MP because his wife helps him to write his speeches. She underplays her suggestions, saying that her notes are 'just trifles – things I was to suggest to you – while I was knitting – and then if you liked any of them you could have polished them'. But then, after he ditches her for a trophy girlfriend, he loses his 'neat way of saying things' because his best phrases have all come from his wife. He finally realises that his career cannot survive without her. At the end of the play, she tells him: 'It's nothing unusual I've done, John. Every man who is high up loves to think he has done it all himself; and the wife smiles, and lets it go at that. It's our only joke. Every woman knows that.'

Only occasionally did Marilyn have to remind me of this story, because I freely acknowledged that she was the force behind everything I did. She encouraged me to be more than I ever imagined I could be.

There were times when she ambushed me with ideas. When she went to the BBC for a meeting and heard that they were looking for a history play on a big subject for Easter, she said, 'I'll get James to write a play about Bach.' When a bibliophile told her that five out of the six assistants on Dr Johnson's dictionary were Scottish, Marilyn turned to me and said, 'That's a play.' And when my novel, *East Fortune*, sold badly and I couldn't imagine how I would ever make a living from writing, she said that perhaps we needed to think completely differently about my work.

She was directing John Mortimer's *Rumpole of the Bailey* at the time, and we wondered about the secret of its popularity. What would it mean to write a similar series with a lovable central character, someone like my dad, perhaps? And so, eventually, the clerical detective Sidney Chambers came into being and *The Grantchester Mysteries* began. Originally this was set in Westminster Abbey, but Marilyn said, 'No, no, make it Cambridge, where you were born. You know about that.'

I started to write it, chapter by chapter, and Marilyn would then either pencil notes all over the manuscript, telling me what to cut, clarify or expand, or she would send me an email full of ideas. By Book Three, she would even add passages of her own to give me the notion of where I needed more. This was especially true of the scenes between Sidney and his wife because their marriage was, of course, similar to our own.

One story came back with her suggestions in capital letters:

Hildegard was unimpressed when Sidney returned from his lunch at six o'clock in the evening. She was not jealous of Amanda, she told him yet again, AS SHE POINTED THE COLANDER AT HIM IN WHAT COULD ONLY BE DESCRIBED AS AN AGGRESSIVE MANNER, and it wasn't, SHE ASSURED HIM AS SHE RINSED THE VEGETABLES, that she minded them spending so much time together, but he had completely forgotten that they had arranged to have tea with one of the most boring couples in the village. SHE TOOK THE VEGETABLE KNIFE FROM THE DRAWER AS SHE TOLD HIM HOW she had been stranded with them alone FOR ALMOST AN HOUR BEFORE SHE COULD MAKE HER ESCAPE, and ALSO, SHE REMINDED SIDNEY TESTILY, WAVING THE KNIFE AT HIM EMPHATICALLY, he had still done nothing about finding a new curate to replace Leonard Graham, who would have been able to go in his place. SIDNEY TOOK THE VEGETABLE KNIFE FROM HER, KISSED HER, AND SOLEMNLY PUT THE COLANDER ON HIS HEAD.

It was typical of her to suggest a moment of daffiness to add detail and lighten the mood. She also reminded me that *Rumpole* was based on the idea of a triple narrative and that I could replicate this in *Grantchester*. There should be a crime story that was solved at the end of every episode, a character plot that evolved through the series and a comic diversion to provide light relief. The challenge was to establish an authoritative tone that the reader could trust, keep all the different balls in the air at the same time, and build to a satisfyingly unexpected conclusion.

'Simple,' she said, and laughed. Then she kissed me, lightly, on the lips: a blessing and an encouragement.

We spent so many hours reading, writing and talking through ideas that I came to think of my entire marriage as a process of setting out concepts before editing and revising them. It was not just work, it was everything: plans for a meal or a holiday or when we'd see friends or what we'd say to the children.

Previously I had been irritated when I suggested something to my sister Rebecca and she had replied, 'I'll have to check with Christopher.' Then I realised that I did the same thing. Marriage had made me incapable of independent decision-making.

But now that I was alone, there was no one to refer to in the same way, no *companion* to keep me in check and prevent me doing something bonkers, someone who would understand all and forgive all. I had friends, of course, wonderful friends and fabulous daughters, but I didn't have a *wife*.

I tried to imagine the advice that Marilyn would give me if she was still alive. After all, if my marriage of thirty-five years had been so fantastic, I should at least be able to hear her voice in my head. Perhaps I could go on living by pretending she wasn't dead at all? She was away at work somewhere, in London or Glasgow or staying with friends. But then, after a while, I thought, That's enough of that. Time to get back home now. The joke's over.

I found myself coming out with phrases that I had never imagined saying: 'That was before my wife died ... when Marilyn could still talk ...'

On being asked about my marital status, with people assuming that I was divorced, I found myself replying: 'No, I'm a widower ... I *was* married ...'

Then, in a restaurant or at a wedding, I had to find a way of being acceptably single: 'No, it's just me. Don't worry. I'm all right.'

Who was saying these words? They were all emerging from my mouth, but I didn't want to own any of them. Sometimes, I didn't want to talk at all, or even, perhaps, ever again. What could I do about this emptying loneliness?

I didn't want to have to keep going over things, especially the last stages of her illness, or talk about how awful it had all been, but there was nothing else to occupy my thoughts and no way of deviating from her memory because it seemed a betrayal to go on living without her. Happiness was far away but normality was impossible too, particularly at a time when the pandemic meant that there *was* no normality.

I thought about therapy but the last time I had been, only once, a man in a bow tie charged me £360 for a session in which he told me that I reminded him of Stephen Fry.

And so, I decided to concentrate my energies, reduce the number of people I spoke to, and develop an alternative therapy of having one phone call a day at six o'clock with a good friend. I talked to people who were busy and cheerful, theatricals mainly, because they had the ability to make stories, to convert their lives into entertaining anecdotes, to swing between tragedy and farce in the same sentence.

Pip and Siobhán both reported from their television locations, Siobhán telling me that while filming *Midsomer Murders*, 'I've had more Covid tests than I've got lines.' Bill sent me pictures of the 'Bidawee Hand-Knitted Home Studio' he had created in his spare room to record the voice-overs for *The Repair Shop*. 'The commute's a nightmare.'

Julie sent me a cookery book, Signe Johansen's *Solo*, with its subtitle *The Joy of Cooking for One*. I tried out the recipes for 'one-pan wonders' and 'easy week-night suppers'. I concentrated on making simple things with the best ingredients from our local farm shop. Marilyn had always believed in freshness, plenty and simplicity: a bowl of radishes, new asparagus, lemon sole with a tomato salad, the first of the raspberries from Fife.

I remembered praising her when my parents came to dinner, and she said to me: 'I just threw it all together and Bob's your father-in-law.'

On Sunday nights I had scrambled eggs with chives on toast as we had always done. It seemed to mark the end of the week. Now it might as well have been the end of the world. I read the letters of consolation that came after Marilyn's death and couldn't always finish them. One, like this, took several goes to get through, partly because it contains a story I did not know and I felt guilty I had not heard of it. It was from our friend Anna:

Dearest James

How to start? It seems absolutely unfathomable that Marilyn has gone. I can honestly say without qualifications or exaggerations that she was one of the loveliest people I, we, have ever known. Her tremendous, generous warmth just beamed out, like rays from a sun. And her so lightly worn wisdom. I remember her telling me about when one of your children were small and naughty, the key was never to hold annoyance or punishment over them. When they threw the boiled egg on the floor, she said, tick them off soundly, but the next morning make another one and make no reference to the previous day's eggy incident. I have thought of it often — both with babes and grown men — and it has always made me smile and think of Marilyn. How lucky we were to know her, we just a little really, you and your family so profoundly. It is a towering injustice that so many of the best people of all get snatched so soon but then I always think that a day of them, of Marilyn, is worth a decade, a lifetime of so many others, that that is just our lot. Like truffle oil or the loveliest scent, we are treated to only a little, too little of the most wonderful things.

The letters kept on coming. This was from Stuart:

Dearest James

There's a sentence attributed to Ovid. 'Could we see when and where we are to meet again, we would be more tender when we bid our friends goodbye.' One of the most wonderful things about Marilyn was that she always bid goodbye with great tenderness — from the first time of meeting her and you in that curry house in Wantage to the last time of seeing her in the baggage hall of Terminal 5, it was always her way. That was and is miraculously special.

And there was this from George:

All we want is for you to know how much we love you and Marilyn, a woman of oak and of gold. We are here for you always. George.
As I write that I can hear her saying my name in her special way. And it breaks my heart. How I shall miss her. She was a STAR. Her light shall never be extinguished.

Her husband, Crispin, ended his letter very simply:

I so loved and respected Marilyn and will miss her sweetness, perceptiveness and dynamism – such a unique and wonderful combination.
So loved.
Like you are, by me, always.

They were beautiful and saddening letters, written in pen and ink on nice stationery, made all the more moving because they were instinctive and direct. People had set aside time from their daily lives and taken care and trouble to write properly.

Reading them made me want more. I started to go through boxes of old love letters, written before the days of email, when Marilyn and I were first together. I found two hearts that she had drawn and cut out.

The first said: 'J'aime James.'

The other held the words: 'Nous nous aimons.'

Then she continued: 'We need not only to love, and be loved, but to know that we are loved. The realm of silence is large enough beyond the grave.'

Marilyn always wrote straight from the heart: 'I do hope, and now <u>trying</u> to pray again, that our love and faith in one another won't ever wither. I think that it would be the saddest thing ever in my life – I hope I will never disappoint or distress you by anything I might do. You must help me to be more open, braver, to trust myself more. I need you for all these reasons, but most of all I need you because I love you and love you loving me. I'll talk to you tonight …'

How much would I give for one more of those conversations? I thought of all the times I had distressed and disappointed *her* and whether I had ever been a good enough husband. Too late now. All too late.

Dwelling on guilt and misery was not doing me any good but sometimes I could not help but pick away at the scab. Grief became every resting thought.

I looked up the letter the clergyman Sydney Smith wrote to Lady Georgiana Morpeth in February 1820, listing twenty pieces of advice to help his good friend overcome a bout of depression: 'Make the room where you commonly sit, gay and pleasant; be as much as you can in the open air without fatigue; don't be too severe upon yourself, or underrate yourself, but do yourself justice. Short views of human life – not further than dinner or tea.'

I decided to draw up my own version of coping: even thinking of what Marilyn would have done if I had died instead of her.

What would she do, I thought, if she was with me now?

In St Monans we would sit together and watch the light change over the sea and remember holidays in the south of France, Ischia or the Venetian lagoon. On a warm day you could even imagine the Firth of Forth as the Bay of Naples, with Berwick Law as a mini-Vesuvius. There would be the newspapers, or a new novel or a collection of poetry. She might like a glass of cold champagne. We could go to the fishmonger and buy a piece of hake and wrap it in tinfoil with butter, lemon, capers and white wine.

I forced myself to keep the house tidy and engaged in therapeutic cleaning and angry hoovering. I bought nice soap and talc and new cologne and lit scented candles. I polished my shoes and put on my best outfits as Marilyn would have done. I changed the bedlinen and sprayed our bedroom with her perfume. I tried, as my father had always recommended, to 'keep cheerful'. I did this by listening to banging pop anthems or to Bach cantatas, all played very loudly.

Sometimes Bach proved to be too much. I remembered a story about a man weeping uncontrollably in a car park. When asked by a stranger if he was all right, he replied, 'I'm listening to Bach,' and the stranger said, 'That explains it.' I realised the composer's genius was to create a bridge, often in a single piece of music, that stretches from the deepest sorrow to the most exhilarating joy.

I decided I had to work at grief and to keep attacking it even if there were times when I had to submit to its relentless grip and treat it as the price we pay for love. I kept as busy as I could. I tried to imagine Marilyn encouraging me and telling me that it was all right, she was still with me and always would be. We couldn't let a stupid thing like death defeat us. I could do this. I could survive all this pointless emptiness.

Be Marilyn.

That's what I had to do now.

Shouting at Television

I missed watching television together. We often put on cosy crime to escape the strange news agenda of terror and sentimentality. ('The world's going to end, we're all going to die, but, in the meantime, while you're watching, here's a piano-playing kitten.')

Whenever we turned on to *Poirot*, or *Death in Paradise* or *Midsomer Murders*, Marilyn would provide a running commentary on the plot and the actors. She always anticipated the twist, spotted the murderer and called her spoilers out loud. 'The housekeeper's their birth mother … oh God, it'll be the doctor again … it's the cleaner, like the postman in Sherlock Holmes … they're not husband and wife: they're brother and sister. It's Anna Chancellor. It has to be. Otherwise, she wouldn't be in it.'

Sometimes we would already know the criminal because our friends were in the show. Pip was a villain in the ITV series *Heartbeat*, Deborah bumped her patients off in Alan Bennett's *Hallelujah* and Siobhán played twins in *Sea of Souls* which is always a giveaway. It's also a truism that the least famous person is the victim and the most highly paid actor either did it or will be the glamorous red herring. Witness Richard Attenborough in the original production of *The Mousetrap* (the famous actor, even if he's playing the policeman, has to be the murderer). Harriet Walter warned us that she is 'always the red herring' until that proved to be not quite so true in *Killing Eve* in which she trained assassins.

Shouting at the television was not confined to crime. We also liked the ridiculousness of eating ready-meals to watch *MasterChef* and heckling the contestants: 'Life's too short for jewelled Persian rice!' Or 'Not another bloody velouté.' We watched *Gardeners' World* on Friday nights and would shout back at Monty Don as he described his Paradise Gardens or a particularly delicate bit of planting: 'Try doing that in Fife, mate!'

On the night after Marilyn died, I watched the programme with Rosie and Charlotte. It featured an 87-year-old man who was sure he had 'ten more years of gardening still in him' and we all shouted out at exactly the same time: 'Oh fuck off, you bastard.'

On these days of grief and anger, I was filled with fury towards everyone except Rosie and Charlotte. I came to hate smiley photographs of newly engaged couples drinking cocktails on Instagram; text messages that ended with the word 'Hugs'; a perfectly innocent grandmother, the same age as Marilyn, pushing a pram in the street; stick-thin drug addicts outside the methadone clinic refusing to die. Why were they still alive when my wife was not?

When we met the neighbours in the public gardens, they told us they were getting the Covid vaccine 'next week'. The man was going to be eighty on Sunday and so it was 'quite a relief'.

After they had left us, Rosie said, 'Is it just me or did you feel visceral hatred towards them?'

It wasn't just us. I checked with my friend Rachel, who had been widowed two months before me, and she texted back: *Any 'older' couple wandering along holding hands and I'm ready to spit at them.*

I watched David Byrne's *American Utopia* concert and when it came to my favourite song, 'Once in a Lifetime', I found myself no longer wondering how indeed did I get here, and what my life was about, and thought instead: Where has it all gone? How did any of this happen?

I saw a repeat of the sitcom *Mum*, with Lulu and the Lampshades singing the theme tune 'You're Gonna Miss Me When I'm Gone', and shouted out, 'YES I DO.'

I realised that the 'stages of grief' – shock and denial, pain and guilt, anger and bargaining, depression, reconstruction, acceptance and even hope – were not 'stages' at all. They could all happen at the same time, or at least on the same day. They were like the weather. You never quite knew what you were going to get next.

I wondered if I should have done something more to prepare for this, the Johnsonian 'calamity' of the death of a wife. I remembered teaching at the Arvon Foundation and meeting a woman who had just lost her mother. She stood beside her father at the crematorium, and he said to her: 'I've been waiting all my life for this.' The line is pure Chekhov in that it is both comic ('I am rid of my wife at last') and tragic ('I've always dreaded this feeling of loss and abandonment') at the same time.

My friend Beth phoned me from France to ask how I was and said that the longer I talked to her the more dread she felt. Both her parents were still alive. 'I know it's coming for all of us.'

It's not as if we hadn't been warned. Marilyn's father had always told her whenever she complained about anything: 'Life's tough and then you die.' When she was a little girl, Siobhán's mother said to her: 'You die alone, so you have to learn to live alone.' And I was brought up in a vicarage where the Book of Common Prayer provided a constant reminder that death could come at any time.

I wasn't christened by my father, but by his friend Lancelot Fleming, who was known for his saintly absent-mindedness. He began my service of baptism thus: 'Man that is born of a woman hath but a short time to live and is full of misery. He cometh up and is cut down like a flower; he fleeth as if it were a shadow, and never continueth in one stay.'

'Lancelot,' my father interrupted, 'that's the funeral service.'

Perhaps this is why I came to write detective fiction. My life began with a funeral. And I have a theory that crime writing has displaced religion in the West to become the secular space in which we address our deepest fears and anxieties.

A hundred years ago, in the United Kingdom, people used to recite the Book of Common Prayer at least twice a day, at morning and night: 'Good Lord, deliver us from lightning and tempest, from plague, pestilence and famine; from battle and murder, *and from sudden death*.'

Now, in a less Christian world, perhaps the most frequent way we think about the human condition is through crime fiction and drama. It allows us to think safely about death and look for the consolation, justice and closure that is found wanting in real life.

Death is, of course, the great subject. Mortality fires our search for meaning. In February 2021, the BBC repeated a film about Keats's final journey to Italy that I had made in 1995 with Andrew Motion. It had marked the 200th anniversary of the poet's birth. Now, twenty-five years later, it was the 200th anniversary of his death. We hired an old Lowestoft fishing smack, the *Excelsior*, seventy-seven feet long with dusty red sails, and Andrew read from Keats's letter to his friend Brown about his great love for Fanny Brawne, written aboard ship in 1820: 'The thought of leaving Miss Brawne is beyond everything horrible – the sense of darkness coming over me – I eternally see her figure eternally vanishing. Some of the phrases she was in the habit of using during my last nursing at Wentworth Place ring in my ears – Is there another Life? Shall I awake and find all this a dream? There must be. We cannot be created for this sort of suffering.'

When we got to the house in Rome where he died, I sat on his bed and looked at the daisies carved on the ceiling and remembered how Keats had said that he thought they were the flowers growing over his grave. The curator of the Keats–Shelley Association asked me if I would like to see Keats's death mask. She took it out of its case and gave it to me. She let me hold his head in my hands. It was cold and small and white. I thought of the lines from *Hyperion*:

> *Then saw I a wan face,*
> *Not pin'd by human sorrows, but bright blanch'd*
> *By an immortal sickness which kills not;*
> *It works a constant change, which happy death*
> *Can put no end to; deathwards progressing*
> *To no death was that visage; it had pass'd*
> *The lily and the snow …*

I held the face of Keats and I did not want to give it back. But I had to. I had to wake from the dream – but even then, I was filled with that most Keatsian of sensations, the feeling that transient, fleeting, poetic and transcendental moments are but glimpses of eternal rest – and that, in Wallace Stevens's famous phrase, 'death is the mother of beauty'.

I watched the film again and could hardly believe I had made it. It was slow and elegant and overproduced. Any television executive now would have told me to get a move on; but I was proud of its grace and beauty, its music and photography, its confidence to take its time and be poetic. It asked viewers to stop their hurrying lives. After I had seen it once more, this evidence of a former life, I stepped into the street and couldn't believe the noise and the bustle, even in lockdown, and what seemed to be nothing less than the sheer banality of everyday existence. I looked at people going about their business, putting on their masks at the bus stops, calling out random greetings and farewells, and wanted to shout and swear at them all over again: 'What are you doing *shopping*, for God's sake?'

I remembered the Book of Lamentation from the funeral service and sent the verse to Rosie. *Is it nothing to you, all ye that pass by? Behold, and see if there be any sorrow like unto my sorrow, which is done unto me, wherewith the LORD hath afflicted me in the day of his fierce anger.*

This was the strange paradox of grief. We think it is unique to us and yet it is common to all.

I looked at a little black notebook Marilyn had given me with 'Inspirations and Ideas' gilded on the cover. Inside she had written 'For my beloved James' and quoted from Raymond Carver's 'Late Fragment'. I started it in Istanbul, on our last holiday together, with our friends Bill and Hildegard, Jo and Stuart, and it contains notes from exhibitions and ideas for novels. It begins with what

Henry James called a *donnée*, the germ of an idea, based on the fact that we were there on St Andrew's Day, the patron saint of Scotland. With the town of St Andrews being just by our home in Fife, Bill and Marilyn had the notion to go on a series of holidays that would collect his scattered relics until we had seen the whole body – his main relics in Amalfi, Italy; his skull and a finger in Patras, Greece; his shoulder in Edinburgh; his arm in Cologne; and another 'small relic' in Kiev.

Then there were notes for a series of stories concentrating on human anatomy – the pianist's hand, the actor's voice, the alcoholic's liver; the lover's lips, the raised eyebrow, the fingerprint. I planned a novel based on different parts of the human body and had the idea to structure it around Rembrandt's painting of *The Anatomy Lesson of Dr Nicolaes Tulp* until a quick internet search informed me that Nina Siegal had already spent six years doing this.

'Never mind,' Marilyn told me. 'You'll have more ideas. You just have to keep thinking them up.'

And then the notebook changed: gone were the ideas and instead came the hastily written reminders of problems, phone calls, things I had to do: 'Choking, thick saliva, nebuliser unit, community nutrition team, key info summary, oral antibiotics. Call Duncan Reekie re St Monans grave. Fife Council burial plot.'

After that it ran out. There were only blank pages.

I was going to have to think how to fill them again.

With this.

We're Not Really Here

Halloween.

There was a fierce wind off the sea in St Monans, the lightweight table I should never have ordered was thrown across the garden, its base broken and the chairs scattered. The plants were scorched by wind and sea salt. It was as if the local poltergeist had been at it again.

A blue moon hung low in the sky. Marilyn's brother was born on a similar night and it is the defining anthem of the football club I support, Manchester City, a team that played attractive free-flowing football in the sixties when I was growing up. We even had 'Blue Moon' sung at our wedding.

The children gave me a Manchester City shirt for my fiftieth birthday, with RUNCIE 10 on the back. In 1968, when I was nine years old, my parents put blue-and-white icing on my birthday cake and gave me the away kit so I could imagine playing for them when I did a kickabout in the back yard.

'It's Corrigan, he throws the ball out to Book, Book passes inside to Doyle, Doyle to Bell who finds Summerbee. It's back inside to Lee, and now Runcie's making a run. Runcie has the ball, it's 1–1 in the last minute of the cup final, he cuts inside, he goes past Bremner, he goes past

Hunter, it's on to his right foot, he shoots, AND RUNCIE SCORES, what a goal!'

No one can quite understand this passion for a team for whom I have no natural affiliation. I had never lived in Manchester. My father supported Liverpool. I should have been a fan of Oxford United when I was a boy, or Watford as a teenager, because that was where we lived. But it was always City, for all their glamour and their failings, their champagne swagger and their inability to defend. I also love them for their sense of humour, joshing the well-dressed José Mourinho with a chant of 'Your coat's from Matalan' or commemorating one of the Manchester United player Wayne Rooney's latest conquests with 'He's fat, he's red, he'll take your gran to bed.'

In the dark days of the early nineties and the early noughties they ended up, temporarily, in what was technically Division 3. This was also when one of their most iconic songs, sung to the tune of 'We Shall Not Be Moved', came to the fore. It's 'We're Not Really Here'.

We are not, we're not really here
We are not, we're not really here
Just like the fans of the Invisible Man
We're not really here.

It was considered unbelievable that a team with such a trophied history should be forced to play at York City, Chesterfield and Lincoln, where the chant may have been first heard after a shock defeat in 1996. The team really were, at times, very bad indeed. (I watched a particularly grim 0–0 draw with Crewe Alexandra and so yes, to quote another chant, 'I was there, I was there, I was there when we were shit.')

At home in St Monans, I watched City played Olympiacos on television. It was 3 November 2020, the night of the American election. The Etihad stadium was empty of fans due to Covid and the banners across the seats read 'We're not really here'. So, this was a kind of reverse. The people were absent, they were not there, but they were watching on television and were being quoted as if they were both there and not there at the same time.

This existential freefall is, perhaps, the nature of what it is to be a writer or, like Marilyn, a director. You have to be inside a scene, watching and observant, and at the same time you have to be anonymous. You can't intrude or make it part of your ego. The characters should appear to play each scene independent of direction but be natural and unpredictable as if everything is happening live every night. As a writer and a director, you are part of the process but have to pull back. You are both there and not there. 'We're not really here.'

Henry James wrote about this; how writers need to be both present and absent at the same time; how they must dominate their material and yet let go to give the characters room to inhabit the story. In *The Private Life*, the playwright Clare Vawdrey only truly exists when he is alone, sending out a doppelgänger when he is in company; while the gregarious socialite Lord Mellifont completely disappears when he has no one to talk to. There are times when neither of them is really present, creating different versions of themselves in the theatre of everyday life. Lord Mellifont 'was all public and had no corresponding private life, just as Clare Vawdrey was all private and had no corresponding public one'.

There is a gulf between privacy and performance, the private and the public self, and Henry James is asking: 'Which is real?' And there are times when I wonder when I am most myself and if the person showing off at a literary festival is really me or even a person I'd like to be. Even writing this memoir, rather than a novel, I have to think if I am really being honest and truthful. Sometimes I am embarrassed to be the 'James' I show to the world, a public version that, like everyone, has an underlying nervousness and anxiety. I know that I only really feel at home not so much in a physical space, but when I am alone with Marilyn in bed at the end of the day, and I don't have to worry about anything any more because she is there and we can talk and nothing matters apart from each other.

Except now she isn't.

Or is she?

Perhaps I have disappeared too. Like Lord Mellifont in the Henry James story, I have 'no corresponding private life' or at least no love life except in memory and the imagination.

My sister used to say to me: 'It's so hard to know what Marilyn really thinks.' There were times when she would, indeed, put on a social performance or be excessively 'polite' to someone she disliked. But it *was* easy to tell what she thought when you learned to read the signs, though she hated confrontation. She would always try to deflect it, or put it off, or hope it would go away if she left it long enough (whereas I always like a bit of a barney).

In more tedious situations, she would keep on asking questions in the hope that the person speaking would be so unusually boring that they would paradoxically become interesting: a dinner-party guest explaining how a fax machine worked, a plane-spotter at a wedding talking through the technical details of Gatwick Airport's departure board, a woman insisting that a suitcase could only be used eighteen times before it wore out. These people didn't always come out the other side to be worthy of anecdote and, when they didn't make the cut, there were post-mortems on the way home when Marilyn would rant at me and shout that 'they were confusing me with someone who gives a fuck'.

She always was what her friend Georgia calls 'a champion swearer'. On our twentieth wedding anniversary, Marilyn gave me two prints modelled on Penguin book covers. The first dustjacket reads: 'Fuck Art, Let's Dance.' The second says: 'Fuck Dancing, Let's Fuck.'

But, in company, she wanted to be kind and for the party to be gay, and to bring out the best in people; in me, her family and those she worked with. She was always pushing people to think creatively and to do more than they thought they could.

This social wondrousness could be hard to keep up, even exhausting at times, but I think this was one of Marilyn's greatest professional achievements — to be entirely responsible for a show and yet *to appear absent*. It's a bit like parenting. You parent a child, you parent a show, and eventually you have to let go of them both.

We're not really here.

But you are, of course, and perhaps it's enough that you know and, in reality, they know too.

When the City fans sing 'We're Not Really Here' they are defiantly asserting that they *are*, in fact, present. They are bloody well there. Another possible origin of the song comes from the idea that City fans managed to infiltrate the infamous Den at Millwall when away fans were banned and sang it there — but this seems unlikely bravado. However, I quote this now because Marilyn was a great admirer of the chant 'We are Millwall Super-Millwall. No one likes us. We don't care' because it is sung to the tune of Rod Stewart's 'Sailing' and Rod Stewart albums are what everyone's Scottish dad used to get for Christmas.

Although Marilyn never quite got the point of football, she understood the idea that it was unscripted theatre, that a manager such as Pep Guardiola, like a drama director, would have to wrangle a cast including stars and egos, make individuals play as a team, and be responsive to setbacks, weaknesses and unexpected defeats.

And she always 'got' the drama of cup runs, minnows versus giants, and the grim humour of the sign in the back of the bus in 1975 when Scots fans returned from Wembley after a 5–1 defeat to England with the taunt: 'You couldnae make it six.'

One of her favourite stories was to tell of the infamous exchange between the radio commentator David Francey and television's Archie Macpherson at a Scotland away game in Hungary. Francey knew that he wouldn't be able to remember every Hungarian footballer and so asked his colleague to let him know the correct name if any of them scored.

They did.

In the midst of the chaos, panic and excitement, Francey asked Macpherson who had hit the back of the net.

'Fucked if I know,' came the reply.

So Francey picked up his microphone and uttered the immortal words 'Yes, it's that man, FUCTIVANO' to his startled listeners.

She loved this story and its opportunity for more 'champion swearing'. She was thrilled by the theatrical heat of improvising on the spot to disastrous effect, but the idea of giving it a go, throwing yourself into things and being an enthusiast lay at the heart of her personality. The idea of delight, of being in the moment, and a *true supporter*, lay behind Marilyn's idea of parenting, friendship, direction and love.

One of the writers she worked with most frequently was Michael Chaplin and their last production together was *For the Love of Leo*, a radio drama series about a widower in Edinburgh searching for love after the death of his wife and her funeral in Canongate Kirk. The ghost of the wife, played by Beth Marshall, even talks him through the future candidates and the memories of their marriage.

Listening, or rather trying to pay attention without quite being able to face up to it, I couldn't help but feel: 'For God's sake, this is ridiculous. Marilyn does know I'm listening to this, doesn't she?'

For this to be Marilyn's last production and for a third series to be made after her death and from beyond the grave? I wondered what I was supposed to think. Was this her chance to talk back to me, her way of dealing with anticipatory grief, of going first, even a kind of revenge for the anticipatory grief in my fiction in which loving, generous women with beautiful voices are either redeeming the hero (me) or dying to leave them bereft (also me)?

But then, I had to remember, this series on Radio 4 was not actually about me. It was a drama by Michael Chaplin who, presumably and amazingly, didn't think about *me* at all when he wrote it. And despite all the attention it got, and the love for Marilyn that was shared on Twitter about the production after she died, I couldn't help but feel disorientated. *My wife*, if you don't mind. And yet, and yet, it also became a haunting and a comfort. She was both present and absent, like the characters in the Henry James story, a friendly ghost.

I thought of all those films with the guiding presence of the dead over those left behind: Patrick Swayze in *Ghost*, Alan Rickman in *Truly, Madly, Deeply*, and, perhaps more accurately, Elvira in Coward's *Blithe Spirit*, blowing in through the French windows and wrecking any chance of a second happiness.

I think I'd rather you just had a string of affairs with women who can't possibly live up to me.

I thought of this business of absence and presence, of Halloween and ghosts and hauntings. At Halloween I imagined I was living in a ghost story that everyone else had read and that no one had told me about.

I watched football without her and was intrigued by the collapse in form of the champions, Liverpool, deprived by Covid of the Anfield crowd to roar them on and 'suck in' the extra goals. There was an article about their manager, Jürgen Klopp, and how he surely wanted to tell everyone: 'You do know that this isn't real football?' It's a pale imitation. It's not the same game without the supporters, and I started to think that this was an exact metaphor of my life because all its special atmosphere had been removed too: *You do know that this isn't real life?*

There is, at times, a giddiness to grief. You feel a recklessness after the worst has happened. The house can burn down, you don't care about personal ambition and 'nothing really matters', to quote 'Bohemian Rhapsody'. You have been given a bizarre freedom.

To continue with the football analogy, it's as if you're in an existential version of extra time; or it's as if you've already been relegated and can play as attacking a game as you like because you have no defence and the result doesn't count. I watched West Bromwich Albion, doomed to the championship, beat the mighty Chelsea 5–2 because they had abandoned all hope and played with all the brilliance of 'having a laugh'.

I planted daffodils and had to go back to the garden centre for more earth. 'I don't know why I'm doing this,' I told Phyllis, Fife's blue-eyed queen of bulbs and bedding. 'Sometimes, I can't see the point if it's just for me.'

'It's for her too,' she said. 'She's watching you. She'll know.'

But is she? I wanted to ask.

We take comfort in the idea that the dead are watching over us. You can just about see our house from the graveyard, and I know she's facing in the right direction. That's what Alan, the undertaker, told me.

'She can see you. Don't you worry about that. You think I'm joking?'

So, I thought of what it might be like not to be haunted, but to be accompanied. To have a happy ghost as it were, a blessed ghost, someone who was there and not there.

'I'm not *really* here.'

But you are.

May Her Memory Be a Blessing

Working in the media is often hypocritical nonsense. It never ceases to amaze me how people responsible for the most sensitive programmes about art, love, joy and beauty can still be total bastards. My friend Jamie was made redundant at the BBC in the days between his mother's death and her funeral. The Head of Music and Arts acknowledged: 'I know it's not a good time for you, but we can't wait. Sometimes these things have to be done.' His main aim ('we can't wait') was to get it all over and done with as quickly as possible. At another time, my friend Joanna, a pianist, had to cancel a day of filming after her mother-in-law's death and was told: 'Why can't you just move the funeral?'

We live in an age where the unbereaved have little awareness of what loss is like. Only a month after Marilyn died, I received a text from a colleague hoping I was feeling 'a bit better'. Rosie told a friend she had been depressed and was asked: 'Oh, have you had a bad week?'

Then a very kind woman I don't know well wrote to say: 'You must feel you have lost half of yourself.'

Must? Half? No. *All sense of myself. All of it.* I do not know who I am any more without her.

In the past, grief was more visible. There were mourning practices, customs, rules. Cassell's *Household Guide* from the 1880s takes the reader through four sections of 'Death in the Household', including instructions for the most ostentatious of ceremonies: 'Funeral costing £53: hearse and four horses, two mourning coaches with fours, twenty-three plumes of rich ostrich-feathers, complete velvet covering for carriages and horses, and an esquire's plume of best feathers; stout outside lead coffin, with inscription plate and solder complete; two mutes with gowns, silk hat-bands and gloves; fourteen men as pages, feathermen, and coachmen, with truncheons and wands …'

There was a sumptuary aspect to lamentation. Queen Victoria had black tears stitched into her handkerchiefs and helped Courtaulds to a fortune in the manufacture of black crêpe. If I had been grieving in Victorian times, people would have been able to tell just by looking at my hat-band: 'The width of the hat-bands worn differs according to the degree of relationship. When worn by the husband for the wife they are usually at the present time about seven inches wide. Those worn by fathers for sons, and sons for fathers, are about five inches wide. For other degrees of relationship, the width of the hat-band varies from two and a half inches to four inches.'

The consolation of religion is strangely absent. Instead, this is an advertisement for grief, a shopping opportunity, a chance to go to Jay's Mourning House (founded in 1841) for nineteenth-century retail therapy and stock up on all kinds of clobber: veils of crêpe and dresses of parramatta, mourning caps lined with white lace, plastrons edged with rows of dull black beads, all to show – well, exactly what? That you are respectable, that you know how to behave, that you feel deeply. You love and have suffered and are behaving well and in accordance with decency. A modern pin simply says 'Please be kind to me, I'm grieving' which is a more minimalist way of doing things.

The Victorians viewed mourning with dramatic inevitability. You have been warned. Now, it's here. You have arrived in death's waiting room at last. It reminds me of my father telling me that one of his parishioners was 'in the departure lounge'. When it came for his own turn to die, he said to me: 'I know I'm at the gate. The best we can hope for is that the flight's delayed.'

We no longer live in the Victorian era and so we have to find a modern manner of mourning. How can we acknowledge death, talk about it and be kind to each other? What will be most helpful? There is bereavement counselling, therapy, faith, routine and memorialising (this book). There are visits to the grave, a favourite place, letter writing, conversations on the telephone, walks with friends. There is Time, *the great healer*. Time, with a capital letter. Time, that, we are told, makes everything more bearable: *This too shall pass*. But it doesn't look like passing.

There is no formality to grief. Some days pass well enough apart from the odd *bouleversement*, the half-hour gusts of inexplicable melancholy and the bursting into tears when a song comes on the radio (Bastille's 'Good Grief', Adele's 'Hello', Bob Dylan's 'I Want You', the Script's 'If You Could See Me Now', Paloma Faith's 'Only Love Can Hurt Like This').

Picking up a book by Susan Stewart, *On Longing* (it seemed appropriate), I found a note Marilyn had left for me:

Tuesday before leaving –
My own darling –

Ways to feel better soon –
Have a long deep sandalwood-scented bath
Sip peppermint tea
Listen to Bach
Look at the lilies
Read Charlotte's note to the tooth fairy by her bed
Remember I love you
M

This was hopeless. I went to see Charlotte, foolishly thinking that because she had a husband and a daughter she would somehow be better adjusted to this; that she might be further down some kind of 'road to recovery', rather than the 'road to nowhere'. But one of her closest friends had died in her sleep at the age of thirty-one, and another had lost a baby when twenty-three weeks pregnant. She told me that she was living in 'a plague of grief', that the Book of Job had nothing on this. I realised that there was absolutely no right way of getting through all the things that the family were feeling. There was no magic cure or best way forward or 'road map back to normality'. There was never going to be any normality again.

Grief is a virus. It keeps mutating.

There was also the problem of insomnia. In bed, and without Marilyn, I was constantly turning to my left and finding no one there. Sometimes, when I woke up in the middle of the night, I tried to pretend that she had gone to the bathroom or was making a cup of tea. She'll be back in a minute, I thought. But she never did come back. I tried to sleep and then dreamt that her death was all my fault and woke again just before five, the exact time she stopped breathing.

I dreamt that she was ill, and we were in St Monans and Andrew Motion came to see us (it must have been the repeat of the Keats film). He asked for some red wine, but we didn't have any. I went out to buy some and the whole landscape changed. I was on the coast, but it was a steep and rocky escarpment. I couldn't get off it. There were some children and I asked them the way to the village shop because nothing was familiar. They told me there wasn't one. I turned back to go home but there were fields in front of me and no sign of any buildings apart from the St Monans Windmill. I thought, Well, that's all right, but our house had disappeared. I asked an old man where it had gone but I couldn't speak, no words came out of my mouth. There was no way I could get back to Marilyn. I was lost. She was with someone else. I was not there. And I was to blame for her dying.

In another dream, I bought an open-topped sports car but it was so low that I couldn't see ahead and shouldn't have been driving. Then the bottom fell off. I was next to a church but, when I tried to call for help, I dropped the phone and that broke too. When a mechanic came, it was Grayson Perry. I asked if I could use his phone to call Marilyn but all the instructions were in Chinese and there was no response to any button I pressed. Then I dropped that phone as well.

I was going mad.

Bizarrely, I wondered if this was perfectly normal. Grief makes you crazy. In the aftermath of Joe Biden's victory in the American presidential election, I looked up all that a man acquainted with sorrow had thought after the death of his wife and daughter: 'For the first time in my life, I understood how someone could consciously decide to commit suicide ... not because they were deranged, not because they were nuts. Because they'd been to the top of the mountain, and they just knew in their heart they'd never get there again, that it was never going to get – never going to be that way ever again.'

After the death of his son, Biden spoke of how you had to get through a year of anniversaries before you could start to recover. I thought of Marilyn's birthday, and our wedding anniversary, and Christmas, and New Year, and Valentine's Day, and Easter, and my birthday, and Charlotte and Rosie's birthdays, and everything that we had been doing in the previous year and how we had to live through all the reminders of the diagnosis, the disease and her death before we could ever think about anything else.

And contemplating 'a year of anniversaries', I picked up Leon Wieseltier's book *Kaddish*, in which he writes about saying the same prayer three times a day, morning, afternoon and evening, in shul, for the year after the death of his father.

He examined the teaching of Nahmanides, the thirteenth-century philosopher whose reflections on mortality were compiled into his *Torat Ha'Adam* or *The Law of Man*, a book that begins with 'a perplexity': 'Since man is destined to die, and deserves to lie down in the shadow of death, why should we torture ourselves over somebody's death, and weep for the dead, and bemoan him? After all, the living know that they will die. It is puzzling that those who know what will come to pass should then mourn, and call others to lamentation.'

Wieseltier learned that sorrow is a form of remorse. Mourning is an act of repentance, a duty to attend to the cares of the world. It is a process of prayer and ritual that leads one to pay more attention in memory than one did in life, to understand that love is strong as death, and to be grateful for the blessed lives that have been lived.

After the twelve months of saying the kaddish every time a mother or father is mentioned, the mourner adds the words: 'May his memory be a blessing for life in the world to come.' Modern Jews have made this simpler: 'May his memory be a blessing' here, upon us.

I thought of Marilyn, and what a gift it was to know her, and I planned to use the phrase every time I spoke her name: *May her memory be a blessing*.

But in the narcissism of grief, this wasn't enough. I wanted to think about her and acknowledge her and pray for her *all the time*. In the midst of the Covid lockdown, I spent so much time alone that I even began to enjoy and depend upon it; a separation from the world.

My life was grief.

Sometimes I worried I was over-remembering the last year to the detriment of previous years. So much suffering, so much pain.

I tried to think positively, that Marilyn's life was about far more than its final year, and that I shouldn't let her memory be defined by disease.

But I couldn't stop remembering how awful it was. And I could no longer hear her beautiful voice as it was. I was obsessed by the end, by her not being able to say anything clearly. What did she mean by 'esh' – was it 'fresh'? But fresh what? And then spelling out letters and not being able to guess what she was saying and then realising there was nothing I could do anyway: 'B-R-E-A-T-H-L ... *breathless*.' How could I help with that?

I started to garden furiously, wearing all my best clothes because I didn't really care about anything any more. I bought some horticultural grit which was nice and some ice-white pebbles which were not. I was about to put them down by the front of the house when I could imagine Marilyn mouthing the word 'vile' as if the word itself was too horrible to say out loud.

The insomnia persisted and in the middle of the night I found myself shopping online for things I didn't need: a set of sushi knives, two Eazi Kleen ear-wax removers, and a shiny silver jacket made out of copper wiring that could only be worn by a grime DJ in East London. I convinced myself Marilyn would say 'Why not?' even though I couldn't hear her saying it.

Then, after I had left St Monans for Edinburgh, ten minutes into the journey I was caught up by traffic and roadworks and was stuck behind a van advertising mobility scooters – *The Best a Gran Can Get!*

For God's sake, I thought.

I let out this sigh, as I often did when this kind of thing happened, and suddenly there she was, sitting beside me again, saying what she always said when she could see that I was tense even though a journey had only just begun.

'Would you like a Softmint?'

Her voice had come back, clear and true, and she was with me once more. Perhaps this was the beginning of some kind of recovery?

Her voice came out of nowhere, in a traffic jam at the bottom of a hill. It wasn't anything profound. It was completely mundane and yet it was also overwhelmingly beautiful and consoling, a practical everyday love, normality returning.

'Would you like a Softmint?'

May her memory be a blessing.

Dr Johnson's Sermon

After the death of his wife on 17 March 1752, Dr Johnson wrote a sermon in her honour which he asked his friend John Taylor to preach. It was composed in the heat of grief, just as he had written *Rasselas* in a week to pay for his mother's funeral. The sermon has an extraordinary fluency, praising his wife's inestimable virtues. But Taylor refused to preach it, finding the celebration of Tetty Johnson's virtues excessive and untrue, telling friends that, far from being a saint, the woman 'was the plague of Johnson's life, was abominably drunken and despicable … Johnson had frequently complained to him of the wretchedness of his situation with such a wife.'

So, what was going on here? Why do the living want to make saints of those they have lost?

The Johnsons' marriage had lasted seventeen years. Elizabeth Jervis Porter was the widow of a mercer and woollen draper with a dowry of £600 a year and three children of eighteen, sixteen and ten. She was forty-six years old when they married (although she wiped six years off on the marriage certificate) and Johnson was twenty-five. Her family could not understand why she would throw away her life, and her dowry, on a penniless man who was more than twenty years younger with few realistic prospects save his literary ambition. He was tall, lean and lank, wore his natural hair rather than a wig, had scrofula scars on his face and according to Lucy Porter, his future stepdaughter, was 'hideously striking to the eye'. He spoke with 'convulsive starts and odd gesticulations' and was prone to introspection and depression. But her mother pronounced: 'This is the most sensible man that I ever saw in my life.'

People could not understand it. The actor David Garrick described Tetty to Boswell as 'very fat, with a bosom of more than ordinary protuberance, with swelled cheeks, of a florid red, produced by thick painting, and increased by the liberal use of cordials; flaring and fantastic in her dress, and affected both in her speech and general behaviour' and she was said to have come from a hard-drinking family. Johnson insisted that it was 'a love marriage upon both sides'.

By her late fifties, however, Tetty avoided his sexual advances, moved out to Hampstead and turned to laudanum, gin and books of romances. She was described by various contemporaries as frail, fearful, drunken and neurotic.

But, in his sermon, Johnson was having none of this: 'Let it be remembered that her wit was never employed to scoff at reason, nor her reason to dispute against truth. In this age of wild opinions, she was as free from scepticism as the cloistered virgin.'

This seems unlikely, but Johnson continued with a defence of his wife that is so bold that any refutation would seem churlish. 'She was extensively charitable in her judgments and opinions, grateful for every kindness that she received, and willing to impart assistance of every kind to all whom her little power enabled her to benefit. She passed through many months of languor, weakness and decay, without a single murmur of impatience …'

This is also improbable …

'… and often expressed her adoration of that mercy which granted her so long time for recollection and penitence.'

I just do not believe this – just as I do not believe the gravestones that say: 'After a long illness, patiently borne.'

But Johnson was determined to define his wife's lasting reputation before anyone else did, ideally as some kind of latter-day saint. He wanted the world to know that she was wonderful, and I realised I had been trying to do this too.

With Marilyn, MND was not exactly 'patiently borne' but she tried even though she was also, by turns, angry and depressed. It may have been *seen* to have been 'patiently borne' when the professional carers came in and she was wheeled to the shower and hoisted from room to room because it made the process easier and she had no choice. But that did not mean she accepted or ever came to terms with the death knell of disease.

She only did not want her character to be corrupted by it. Just as she was determined to be clean and sweet-smelling and well dressed, she wanted her graciousness, kindness and thoughtfulness towards other people to be preserved; and although she could not reply to all the messages of love and goodwill that came to our home, she did send this to her former colleague Gordon House. It was one of the last emails that she was able to write herself:

Dearest Gordon,
Thank you for your lovely card and the very kind words and thoughts within it. It means so much to me. Being thought of

and remembered is everything in this life; it's all we have and all we take with us.

I always remember and often think of your generous and appreciative words and wise and kindly advice over the many years we have known one another.

Thank you for all of that.

With warmest affection,

Marilyn

She wanted to be her best self for as long as possible even though the family found this quite hard to live with. Catherine, her friend and colleague, wrote to me to say that she was not fooled, and she knew what Marilyn was doing, but please could I tell her the truth? So, the girls and I found ourselves keeping up appearances, following what Marilyn wanted, while sometimes betraying her by telling our friends the facts.

At the same time, she would still send out extraordinary responses. Here is one:

Beloved Tom,

What a moving and heart-warming letter … with many thoughts which I have never heard you speak, and which mean so much to me, hearing them so beautifully expressed by you now. This pandemic makes my own health seem not so important in the global scheme of things. I don't feel alone in my predicament and even the prospect of dying is less important; I have had a wonderful life and am blessed in so many ways.

Speaking of blessings, I must tell you how very much your garden videos mean to me. I know, love and remember every inch of your garden, and walking through it with you, hearing the swish of your broad measured strides through the grass, I

am there, and can smell the fresh leaves after rain and the scent
of Sue's cooking from the kitchen, as you and I and James
walk through the prairie with you before lunch. Please keep
them coming; they are balm for the soul; more than ever now.
My enduring love to you and Sue.
Always,
Mxxxxxxxxxxx

Because of these letters some people would tell us that they were pleased she was still working. They assumed the progress of the disease was quite slow and that she might last another couple of years and perhaps they could come and see her after all? And the girls and I would have to say, no, it's impossible.

Some friends thought that we were being difficult, surely the rules of 'not seeing anyone' did not apply to them? And we would say, yes, it really is the same for everyone, Marilyn is not at all well, she does not want to be seen in this state. We would even get annoyed with her when she was publicly brave because we said it was unrealistic. We couldn't keep up the pretence and she would, in turn, be infuriated by us. None of us knew what we were doing. We had had no training for any of this: but we all understood that she wanted her memory preserved at its best.

It reminded me of all the times when I had been most exasperated with her bountiful-hostess saintliness and she would turn to me and say: 'I know, I know. I am impossible. It must be so difficult to be married to me. I don't know why you put up with me. It must be so hard for you. SO hard. God, I can't IMAGINE how hard it must be. Poor you. Poor, poor you, to have a wife like me. I'm just TOO kind, I have too MANY FRIENDS, I am just TOO CHEERFUL, I should be more depressed, more neurotic, more impossible and then I'd be SO MUCH MORE INTERESTING TO LIVE WITH …'

And she would go on and on and on until I had to say: 'Just stop it.'

There were times when the girls complained and she would stand back with her hands on her hips, as if impersonating Tammy Wynette, and quote from the song 'No Charge' in which a mother refutes her little girl's bill for mowing the yard and making her own bed by citing all that she has done for free: giving birth, nurturing her, caring for her when she was ill, loving steadfastly through every setback – *no charge*.

And Rosie and Charlotte would be as infuriated by that as by people saying 'I wish she was my mother' and we would all want to shout: 'SHE IS NOT A SAINT.'

Even Dr Johnson realised that he might have gone too far in the pursuit of his wife's canonisation. 'That she had no failings, cannot be supposed; but she has now appeared before the Almighty Judge; and it would ill become beings like us, weak and sinful as herself, to remember those faults which, we trust, Eternal Purity has pardoned. Let us therefore preserve her memory for no other end but to imitate her virtues …'

And leave the rest to God.

But what is going on here? Why this urge to canonise your late wife? In literature, it's quite common. Milton wrote the sonnet 'Methought I saw my late espoused saint', 'vested all in white, pure as her mind', and Elizabeth Barrett Browning in her *Sonnets from the Portuguese* replaced religious with secular adoration:

I love thee with a love I seemed to lose
With my lost saints – I love thee with the breath

Smiles, tears, of all my life! and, if God choose,
I shall but love thee better after death.

Thomas Hardy, whose first wife Emma Gifford died at the same age as Marilyn, seventy-two, also converted death into divinity. He rewrote the history of their relationship in the famous *Poems of 1912–1913*, going back to the beginning 'as at first, when our day was fair'. Emma was dressed in her 'air-blue gown' and Hardy was trying to relive his relationship all over again, making up for all his mistakes and neglect, appreciating all the best qualities of his wife that he had failed to cherish when she was alive.

Claire Tomalin described the death of Emma as 'the moment when Thomas Hardy became a great poet'. Some eighty poems belong to her. Reading some that were less familiar to me, I found that they could just as well have been about Marilyn.

How she would have loved
A party to-day!
Bright hatted and gloved,
With table and tray
And chairs on the lawn
Her smiles would have shone
With welcomings ...

I can see Marilyn now with her extravagant greetings:'Hello Gorgeousness!', 'Now heaven walks on earth!', 'Tell me good things!'

Yet Hardy's second wife Florence, like Johnson's preacher, was having none of this. 'All the poems about her are a fiction,' she observed, 'but a fiction in which their author has now come to believe.'

Florence Hardy is clearly a stickler for literal rather than fictional or emotional truth. But then if Hardy had been after that, perhaps he would have stuck to prose. What both he and Johnson were creating were acts of reconstruction, mixtures of memory, remorse and creative hope.

It's still a mistake to canonise the dead because it turns them into something they are not, something less human, an idealised apparition. We have to acknowledge that however marvellous our partner may have been in real life, they were no Mother Teresa. Even Mother Teresa wasn't 'Mother Teresa'.

In real life, supposed saints, an ersatz saint, your common or garden saint, is quite difficult to share a home with. Ask their partners. They need to be loved. They are not the ones who cancel the dinner party or give out home truths. They are too preoccupied by being saints. (Like a friend's brother who was 'too busy with the Church' to attend the bedside of his dying mother.) Your duty, if you live with a saint, is to preserve their sainthood. And it can be bloody annoying.

Perhaps if you can't live up to the job the only way of coping is to behave badly and enhance their sainthood. 'I can't help being difficult. I'm married to a saint.'

At one point I decided to talk to my friend Pip about the difficulty of having a 'publicly perfect' wife, because I was convinced that he had one too. 'Of course, it's infuriating,' he told me. 'But that's part of the attraction. If your wife was faultless, life would be boring. Never forget the importance of exasperation in a marriage.'

In his biography of Johnson, Walter Jackson Bate argues the push for his wife's sainthood is eventually due to gratitude. Johnson was forever grateful that, in his youth, she had saved him from penury and madness. She supported him in a way that allowed him to become the man he was. Nothing about her subsequent behaviour could ever erase her initial act of helping him discover his identity.

When a friend asked Marilyn how she put up with me, she smiled and said, 'I just let him get on with it. We both know we'd be lost without each other.'

Well, here I am: lost.

Dr Johnson's way of coping was to hold up his hands, or rather, put them together, and give everything up to God. He then reverts to a kind of blessing: 'Let all remember, that the day of life is short, and that the day of grace may be much shorter; that this may be the last warning which God will grant us, and that, perhaps, he who looks on this grave unalarmed, may sink unreformed into his own!'

It's the traditional Christian conclusion and it has a wonderful rhythm to it, Johnson the lonely cellist playing away at the back of the church when everyone else has gone home.

So why did Taylor not preach this sermon? Possibly to resist hagiography, but also probably because he thought he should say something himself rather than read out a husband's words – or rather the last words.

If you want 'top billing' on a shared gravestone then you die first. If you would prefer to have the last word, then you should organise events so that you die second (and it's probably best not to marry a writer. They always want the last word).

But perhaps we, the living, must continue to honour the dead without making saints of those we have loved. It is an extreme form of humblebragging, a dark and petty thought: 'I may be a bit crap, but my wife wasn't, so that counts in my favour. And by the way, if she was a saint, why do you think she chose me? My wife's a saint and yours is a bit normal and boring. I've loved the most and I've lost the most – so I WIN.'

This rush to saintliness is dishonest regret and I really can't be doing with it. But what is honest regret? What is loving someone and remembering them truly and faithfully? Can you love again, albeit in a different way?

My father once told me that 'it's good to grieve but a sin to hug your grief'. A sin? Or a self-indulgence, an inability to move on – or a desire to protect yourself?

Because, having gone through all this, I worry that if there is 'a next time' or 'a new love', then I will inevitably think: What if she gets MND too? Or Parkinson's disease? Or cancer? Can I really go through all this with someone else?

Then the thought comes: What if I get it? Who will look after me? Will Rosie and Charlotte have to care for me too?

And the answer is: 'Probably, yes.'

For this is what it means to confront the next stage of grief and the inevitability of mortality: 'Do I really want to drag a new love into such desolation? Wouldn't it be easier just to dwell in this one loss, rather than take on the possibility of it happening all over again?'

A friend, who was keen on a widower in the south of France, was rejected with this brutal sentence: 'Anyone who thinks I'm going to love anyone ever again will have to take this ring off my cold dead finger.'

He could, perhaps, have expressed himself more gently. But then grief can be violent as well as quiet and frightened and inward and depressed. It can be used both as defensive armour and as a weapon, an unexploded grenade in a future relationship when you have forgotten that you have already taken the pin out.

I remember a priest once telling me that the key to bereavement was 'time and tears' and it came out so pat that I wanted to kill him, even then, before Marilyn died. Surely, it's more complicated than that? But then again, perhaps it isn't, and time is another kind of privilege.

Rather than being the devourer of our lessening days, perhaps grief is the opportunity to let things fall.

It allows us to acknowledge that while emotions may not falter, and while our feelings may deepen and darken, and the engulfing sadness will inevitably come back to overwhelm us again and again, often when we are least expecting it (seeing a child run excitedly towards her mother in the park, hearing the snatch of an old song), we are reminded that this too will pass; that the dread of transience, the inability to hold on to all that which is good and all that which is lovely also enables us to let go of the pain – if only fleetingly.

We can perhaps take holidays from grief, allow simple pleasures, 'be kind to ourselves' and acknowledge that while those we have loved were not saints, they were people just like us, and we loved them for all of their flaws and all of their glories.

We loved them for their transience, their smile, their laughter, the sound of their voice, the memories we made. We carry them with us through the darkest days, and learn to be honest about the past, realistic about the future and grateful for all that we have known.

That's the aim. But it's still hard.

A Fine and Private Place

On the first Saturday in August 2017, I travelled to Grantchester to open the summer fete. I was very touched to be asked to do this, as I was never quite sure whether they approved of my series of novels set in the village or of the television series that followed. They had enough tourists because of the setting, the proximity to Cambridge and Rupert Brooke's poem 'The Old Vicarage, Grantchester'. The only problem was that I had double-booked myself. I was supposed to be at the Dartington Summer School of Music, in Devon, for the first day of a week's residence. I was not overly worried, as my teaching did not begin until the Sunday, but was alarmed when Marilyn rang me on the train down:

'Did it go well?'

'It went brilliantly, darling. I was introduced as "the hero of our village".'

'And are you drinking white wine after your triumph?'

'I am.'

'Then you need to slow down. You're onstage tonight.'

'WHAT?'

'There's a late-night concert at ten. It's seventeenth-century lute music. You know what lute players are like?

They spend more time tuning than they do playing. Anyway, the performer says he needs eight minutes to tune. Joanna said you would read some appropriate metaphysical poetry to fill for him. She says she'd told you.'

This was my friend Joanna MacGregor, the artistic director. I recalled that she had mentioned it, but I didn't remember that I had actually been 'told'.

'Anyway, you'd better get on the internet and choose some poems. I won't keep you. See you later, darling.'

I started my search. Marvell, Herbert, Donne. I decided to begin with the belter that is Marvell's 'To His Coy Mistress'. I continued to down the white wine for courage and arrived in only just enough time to greet an anxious and serious performer before the concert began. I was ushered on to the side of the stage and looked out to see an audience of some 300 people wondering who on earth I was and what I was doing onstage with a master lutenist.

By the time came for me to 'fill' I thought the only option was, as the Scots in the theatre say, to 'gie it laldy' so I pronounced in my best booming, amused, theatrical, flirtatious voice:

Had we but WORLD enough … and TIME,
This COYNESS … LADY, were no CRIME …

There was a bit of a titter, which I took as encouragement to overact further. Let's have fun, I thought. I can really go to town on this:

My vegetable love should grow
Vaster than empires and more slow;
An hundred years should go to praise

Thine eyes, and on thy forehead gaze;
Two hundred to adore EACH BREAST,
But THIRTY THOUSAND to the rest …

And build to the end:

Let us roll ALL OUR STRENGTH AND ALL
OUR SWEETNESS up into one ball,
And TEAR OUR PLEASURES WITH ROUGH
STRIFE
Through THE IRON GATES OF LIFE …

Dramatic pause:

Thus …

Further dramatic pause:

though we cannot make our sun
STAND STILL,

Knowing smile, increase in volume:

Yet

Last dramatic pause – bring the audience in:

WE WILL MAKE HIM RUN.

Hold position. Smile. Shy little bow. Await applause.
It came.
Afterwards I asked Marilyn if I had got away with it.
'Not too over the top?'

'A bit pissed, but yes, good fun. They loved you.'

'Marvellous.'

'Not as much as I do, though.'

'I know that.'

'My turn, now. That's enough nonsense.'

Two years later we talked about having a sundial in the garden in St Monans. Our friend Lida, a letter-cutter, could perhaps design one for us and we could incorporate the end of the Marvell poem.

> *Though we cannot make our sun stand still*
> *Yet we will make him run.*

It was a symbol of Marilyn's attack on life, the desire to make the best of everything, to appreciate every minute of every day. It was a theatrical determination, a refusal to be bored, a desire to intensify all that we experience, to let nothing pass us by.

I remembered copying out Walter Pater's admonition at the end of his book *The Renaissance*. 'A counted number of pulses only is given to us of a variegated, dramatic life. How may we see in them all that is to be seen in them by the finest senses? How shall we pass most swiftly from point to point, and be present always at the focus where the greatest number of vital forces unite in their purest energy? To burn always with this hard, gemlike flame, to maintain this ecstasy, is success in life.'

But, by the time we approached Lida we already had the death sentence and so we talked to her not just about the sundial but also about the gravestone, and what that too might say. We were reminded of the earlier lines in the poem:

The grave's a fine and private place,
But none, I think, do there embrace.

Lida sent us her designs for the sundial and then for the gravestone, with wild flowers growing around its base. Because it was going to be a shared grave, we decided on our joint profession: *Storytellers*.

Looking at the flowers shown around the foot I remembered Marilyn's love of drawing plants, dating back to botany at school. Whenever we were on holiday she preferred to stop and draw rather than take photographs, even if it was just something in pen and ink that she would fill with watercolour later. The image could be impressionistic, or it could be quite detailed, but she was convinced that this act of observation would help her remember a place far better than if she took a photograph or made notes or kept a diary.

As a result, our home is full of her notebooks and sketchbooks:

Foxgloves at the window, Cuillins beyond, Elgol, July 2012.

Just one of the many seashore plants that grow in the sea walls in Ischia, thick, rounded robust leaves designed to resist salt-water.

July wild flowers, Port Isaac clifftops: coltsfoot, thorn-stemmed bramble, stately cream cowslips, convolvulus, brown dock, marram grass.

Vivid pink alpine flowers growing in the rocks by Loch Coruisk; the plantain, clover and campion meadow at Beauville.

Sometimes, when we stayed with friends, she would paint still lives of the vase of daffodils on the kitchen table, or the pot of geraniums outside the back door. Before and after she died, some of these friends arranged small shrines of the paintings and gifts she had given them. Corners of rooms were dedicated to her memory. They sent me photographs to show how much they were thinking of her. They would always love her, they said. Attention was a kind of prayer.

When Marilyn was alive (there's a phrase I never thought I would write), she took great care and delight in leaving little vases of flowers in the guest bedroom when people came to stay. These were not big formal displays but takings and mementoes from the garden. Now I vowed that I would try and do the same for her. I decided to make 'a graveyard garden' so there would be something fresh and different to bring to the cemetery every week. It would be a task in which I might even find joy, just as she delighted in making her floral arrangements. It would be creative and apposite, a different way of remembering her, constructive and forward-looking, a memorial that mixed hope with beauty.

I started to plan the garden in September, only a few weeks after the funeral, when there was still plenty of colour: pale and rich pink cosmos, deep blue agapanthus, white roses, long-lasting Cape daisies. The Japanese anemones were at their fullest and highest and yet to be toppled by the wind. (For this is a windy garden, right by the sea, not prone to frost but biting winters when an afternoon gale can turn everything brown and destroy all hope and promise until the first snowdrops.)

In October I looked to pink nerines and yellow alstroemeria (even though Marilyn hated yellow flowers she allowed the paler kind along with daffodils in the spring). I picked asters and the last of the white roses and in November there was still some pink flowering hebe, lavatera and rosemary to tie into little sprays.

December was more of a challenge but there were hellebores and cyclamen, red-berried holly and skimmia, cotoneaster and snowberry.

In January there were pink and white heathers, and greenery for Burns Night tied with a tartan ribbon, but it was hard to find arrangements on the days of wind and darkness. I was still waiting for crocus and snowdrop. I planted a mimosa tree because I remembered us going to a New Year's Day concert in Venice and listening to John Eliot Gardiner conduct a series of the great opera arias. But there was no chance of mimosa prospering in Fife in January. The wind shredded all hope off the tree. It had been a ridiculous idea. So I went to the Co-op instead and bought hyacinths and a white orchid.

In March I planned *Iris reticulata* and *Muscari* 'Cupido', and *Senecio* and *Scilla* and white 'Thalia' daffodils. Then there would be the first of the tulips, *orphanidea* or *hageri*, and by April there were her favourite fritillaries, *michailovsky* and *persica*, and pink lily of the valley and the first anemones, *coronaria* 'De Caen'.

I remembered her painting a posy of them that we bought once in France and her saying in our hotel room: 'I love anemones. They die so beautifully.'

Once the bluebells and the peonies and the tulips were up in May, it was going to be a home run for a summer with 'Spring Green' and 'Prinses Irene' and 'Brown Sugar' and 'Queen of the Night'. Then, in June, there were the first white roses, lavender and lilies, honesty and *Ammi majus*; and by July there would be white lupins and foxgloves and 'Ivory Castle' poppies. I tried to grow the same red poppies that we saw in the *Creation* exhibition in 1984, before we were married, the poppies that reminded her of her childhood. There were going to be so many flowers that I thought I could probably take a different posy and lay it on the grave every day. By August there could be sunflowers and sweet peas, freesias and the marguerites. Then it would be the anniversary of her death and another September and another year to think and to plan and learn from my mistakes and appreciate that gardening is about hope.

There was the apple tree she gave me for my last birthday that I shared with her. It is called 'Marilyn' and I thought of the carol, 'Jesus Christ the Apple Tree', that we sang at my father's funeral. My friend Carolyn sent me a link to a concert that she was singing in the Wigmore Hall and without thinking I turned it on and heard her first words and burst into tears:

I will give my love an apple without any core
I will give my love a house without any door
I will give my love a palace wherein he may be
And he may unlock it without any key.

I told Neil, the minister, that there were times when I could not believe that Marilyn had been buried, that those were her mortal remains below ground. He reminded me of what he had said before the funeral: 'She doesn't need her body any more.'

I planted more snowdrops and daffodils and, as I dug and scooped back the earth, getting the soil under my fingernails, I could not help but think: She is in the ground too. And the thought was both unbearable and ridiculous. I found that, when I had finished, I had to go back to the grave and talk to her or be silent, I didn't know which. I hadn't yet learned what you were supposed to do at a grave apart from just stand there and stare into the distance and let the grief come. And so, I gathered up a little bouquet of hebe and pink mallow and rosemary, *that's for remembrance*, and I stood there in our fine and private place and thought of her and the flowers I had planted and the graveyard garden I had planned and all the times that I was going to be with her in the future on this high headland. And then, as I turned to leave on a calm and strangely windless day, with the cold still a long way off, I didn't say goodbye because, I decided, there's no point any more. There is no goodbye, and there never will be. She will always be with me. There will always be a future for a love such as this.

Mindless Tidying

My godmother was a lovely woman called Celia, a hoarder who threw nothing away. I was her lodger for two years at a relatively early stage of her obsession but, even then, the path up the stairs was filled with piles of paper and her bedroom floor was obscured by mounds of clothes and files and notebooks hidden under Indian dustsheets. I used to wonder how she ever found her way to her own bed without slipping or tripping. But I did understand why she never brought any of her romantic interests back home. In the end she did slip, just at the age where the distinction between 'falling over' and 'having a fall' becomes clear. Yet that didn't stop her. One evening we asked the new upstairs neighbour round for drinks. When he went home, we didn't spot that he had left the front door open. Half an hour later the police were round, thinking that something suspicious had occurred. They told us very solemnly that we had been burgled.

'I don't think we have,' said Celia.

The policeman was amazed. 'But can't you see your flat's been ransacked?'

After explaining that our flat was always like this, Celia smiled and confessed to me: 'I'm afraid that's not the first time it's happened.'

It was the spring of 1983 when the Eurythmics had just released 'Who's That Girl?' and I was keen on an appropriate Sloane who was otherwise involved with the minimalist architect John Pawson. Obeying his instructions, she had stripped her flat so that the wooden table at its centre held only a vase of daffodils and a soft Italian leather notebook that was too precious to write in.

It was no way to live a practical life but, when I met Marilyn, I found she was, at least in theory, a great believer in the William Morris idea: 'Have nothing in your house that you do not know to be useful or believe to be beautiful.' And so, when we came to share our lives, we had a joint purge of our possessions in anticipation of Marie Kondo's advice that we should only keep items that 'spark joy'. Unfortunately, this provoked argument rather than delight since, on seeing that we had duplicates, I sent the wrong things to the school sale, most notably a first edition of the Penguin Mersey Poets with its pop-art cover and the vinyl of the Beatles' *Revolver* because I had it on CD and considered that it took up less space.

I was forgiven, just, but it was always brought up in the subsequent years whenever I wanted to throw anything away (I am a great chucker-out). Then, later on in our marriage, we found inspiration and extremity in Michael Landy's Artangel show *Break Down* in which he took over a London store and destroyed everything he owned: all 7,227 of his possessions.

It was February 2001. Charlotte was twelve at the time and we both thought that she should witness this contemporary art 'happening', a literal and philosophical erasure of property, gifts, identity and memory. Michael Landy was at the centre wearing welder's glasses, surrounded by men and women in blue boiler suits breaking down objects into manageable chunks and placing them on a great winding conveyor belt of destruction. And the irony was that it was all taking place in the United Kingdom's Capital of Acquisition: Oxford Street. This was John Lennon's 'imagine no possessions' being enacted. All of Landy's worldly goods were split into ten categories: Artworks, Clothing, Electrical Items, Furniture, Kitchen, Leisure, Perishables, Reading, Studio, Vehicle (his car).

Even the presents that people had given him were there: a Damien Hirst spot paperweight, a Tracey Emin 'Be Faithful to Your Dreams' handkerchief, an Anya Gallaccio mirror, all his memories and photographs. Everything was catalogued, even stuff that should have gone to the dump:

E921: Philips HD4575 – broken cream-coloured plastic toaster with burnt crumbs in catchment tray

E927: Kenwood Cassette Receiver KRC-150L – car stereo with missing detachable face off control panel from Volkswagen Golf CL

E954: Ikea broken white plastic kettle with white electrical flex and moulded three-pin plug

We watched a white T-shirt from Scrapheap Services, with a faded black Jelly Tots sweet wrapper screenprint on the front, pass us on the conveyor belt. His father's old coat. Even his car was broken down. All he had left were the clothes he stood up in.

Now, after Marilyn's death, I was faced with another clear-out, another breakdown.

But what to keep and what to throw away?

First to go were the medicines that had to be returned. Then the medical equipment (all the things that we had only just acquired that had become redundant within weeks: bath chairs, walking frames, commodes, wheelchairs, slings and hoist). The hallway was filled until it resembled a hospital storeroom.

Then, after a few days, underwear, stockings – but it was far too soon for shoes, clothes, dresses, make-up or perfume.

It was the reverse of collecting, this removal. I wanted to de-hospitalise the house and make it normal, but what was normal after a death? How could a house ever be the same again?

Possessions were replaced by absence. The objects that remained had to work harder. Marilyn's treasures had to be brought out and displayed. They might not spark joy, but they were memories, and they could be beautiful once more.

She liked to tidy and make arrangements. It was her way of relaxing, putting things right, placing items *just so*. Perhaps it was a way of exercising control in at least one area of her life when she found everything else chaotic. Start small and work up from there. Most of the time she did it without thinking, as if she was in a kind of dream. The family came to refer to it as her 'mindless tidying'.

We noticed that our friend Hildegard, the designer, did it too, hiding a stray cable, moving a wooden bowl an inch to the left on a table, picking up a glass and putting it next to something else, tutting at the mantelpiece or despairing at a stray sock left on the floor. Marilyn and she were the same – and this abstract and dreamy control-freakery was adopted by her friend Deborah for a performance in Sam Holcroft's *Rules for Living* at the National Theatre. When Marilyn went to see the play, she thought, 'Hang on a minute, that's what I do.' She asked the actress afterwards if she had nicked her mindless tidying. Deborah just smiled and said she couldn't think what her friend could possibly mean.

So, in turn and in tribute, I started to make little displays of flowers and vases and I arranged white china on a shelf as if it was a Hammershøi painting. I looked at interior design magazines which never ever show a television or a computer or a cable and tried replicating their impossible minimalism. Then I looked at one of Marilyn's last arrangements. It was a small collection of leatherbound books, special editions and miniatures, grouped on the chest of drawers in the bedroom: Rossetti's *Goblin Market*, *The Story of Tennyson's 'In Memoriam'*, the Book of Common Prayer, Matthew Arnold's *Selected Poems*, Elizabeth Barrett Browning's *Sonnets from the Portuguese*, Ruskin's *Mornings in Florence*. The pile of books had a simple elegance which I knew she would have found pleasing. I thought of her doing it, I could imagine it all, and there was something indefinably moving about it.

I remembered a letter that Proust had written to a friend in 1913: 'We think we no longer love the dead but then we catch sight of an old glove and burst into tears.'

I became distracted. I found myself carrying socks around the house, looking for the shoes I had worn the previous day. By the time I discovered the shoes, I had put the socks down somewhere else. I couldn't remember where they were and couldn't be bothered to find them. In any case, I couldn't see the point of putting on shoes any more because that might mean going out and facing the world and I didn't want to do that or make another decision.

Then I realised my feet were cold. I needed the bloody socks after all. But should I just put the shoes down again to go and find them because, if I did, would I know where I had left them?

I remembered my mother telling me, 'They're where you left them,' and finding it so irritating.

Then I heard Marilyn's voice, bright and clear, saying, 'Here they are.' She always had a way of walking into a room and finding things that had been staring me straight in the face. I hadn't noticed, and I almost wanted to accuse her of having only just put them there, or of carrying them with her all along, or of deliberately confusing me. But she would just smile and say, 'Look. Here,' and maybe even give me a little kiss and tell me not to get in a state. Everything was going to be all right. There was no need to make a fuss.

Now I remembered all this, I couldn't move. I just wanted her back. All I could do was sit down and cry and think what it was like when she was in the world every day.

This tidying was not sparking any joy at all.

But then I managed to get up and start again and find things that I had forgotten we had given each other. Pens and pencils and notebooks; pillboxes, brooches and compact mirrors; a china plate with a bluebird, a tray for asparagus to be brought out every May, a sugar sifting spoon, a miniature glass vase for floral arrangements. I remembered the look of horror on her face when I gave her a pair of tights as part of her Christmas present one year (I still don't know why I did this) and I tried to get away with it by saying: 'At least it wasn't an iron or a Hoover.'

After her death I found that I was reconfiguring an idea that I had put into one of the *Grantchester* novels, where Sidney and Hildegard wrap up possessions they already had but had forgotten about in order to appreciate them all over again, bringing objects back out into the light.

I moved a picture into the bedroom. It was by Audrey Grant from an exhibition of paintings based on a study of the dancers in Scottish Ballet. Marilyn had chosen an image that wasn't of the dancers but their instructor, observing them like a theatre director, entitled *Standing Figure*. She thought the woman looked a bit like her and she gave it to me for our wedding anniversary in 2014. Now, as I was handling the picture once more, I remembered that she had stuck an observation on the back of the frame:

> *This woman is waiting for the man she loves.*
> *She knows he will be with her soon*
> *She can't wait to see him because she knows that when he appears*
> *Everything will suddenly seem right again, everything possible,*
> *Hope restored; all calm and bright.*
> *She is happy to wait, because he will always return,*
> *Whatever comes between them when they are parted one from the other.*

And then I remembered we had had a bit of an argument about it. I had complained that I was always with her and that all this 'happy to wait' was nonsense because I was the one that did the waiting. She was always so busy that she was never waiting for anything apart from delayed planes and trains.

I remembered going to Istanbul, before the diagnosis, in 2019. We went to see Orhan Pamuk's Museum of

Innocence only to find that it was closed. But we took the novel with us, the story of Kemal's obsessive collecting throughout his romance with Füsun and his creation of a series of exhibits in a museum to her memory. It was filled with his girlfriend's clothes, restaurant menus and old postcards; soda bottle caps, a whisky glass, a sugar bowl, an ashtray, 4,213 cigarette stubs.

At the same time, we remembered Leanne Shapton's intriguing and adventurous photographic novel of evidence, *Important Artifacts and Personal Property from the Collection of Lenore Doolan and Harold Morris*, the story of a love affair told through its memorabilia, catalogued as if everything was up for sale. The reader has to unravel the story of a relationship through the potency of its imagery: an invitation to a Halloween party, the menu for a Valentine's dinner, a photograph of the couple dressed as Benjamin and Mrs Robinson from *The Graduate*, duplicate paperbacks, handwritten notes, photobooth pictures, and then, towards the end, the bill for a restaurant meal where the main course is cancelled and it's all over.

And so, after Marilyn's death, I wanted to do something similar but *in real life* and more focused, to make the kind of arrangements she would have made, to place little objects in the window and create small shrines, keeping everything tidy and seeing if everything out and 'on display' was meant, our home becoming a cross between an art installation and a Museum of Marilyn.

But as I started what might be called *mindful* tidying, I went through crammed and overcrowded drawers and found so much stuff that was hers and hers alone and nothing to do with me. What, for example, should I do with the photograph album of my wife's first wedding when both of them are dead and they had no children?

What do I do about her letters from people other than me? What do I do about my own letters that I have hung on to that I would rather my children did not read? When is the right time to throw things away? How do you curate the life of the one you have lost: and how do you protect and preserve your own personal archive?

I found the tiniest notebook at the back of a drawer with a watercolour of a rose that Rosie had given her and a little inscription she wrote on the day Charlotte was born: 'She is mine to be with and I hope to be what she needs and I can think of no reason why I could ever desert her.'

There was a little pen-and-ink drawing of a statue in Notre-Dame, a watercolour of a Christmas tree and of a couple of dark red poppies with buds she painted at Sissinghurst in 1992. Then there was this:

Two of the many things I love about James Runcie:

The index and middle fingers of his right hand have two small hillocks where pens and pencils over forty years have hollowed out spaces – where all the words he's written have first left their mark on his hand and then the page

Just before James lies down to sleep, he takes off his glasses, with his back towards me, and there are two small clicks – click, click – and the small sound signals his leaving the world of sharp focus and clarity for the world of dreams and me.

I looked out the presents she had given me over the years: a gold chain with a heart and charm initials: M, R, C; the four little Calvados glasses that were my first Christmas present; a brass Mizpah 'sweetheart' brooch dating from the First World War, engraved with the phrase,

'The Lord watch between me and thee, when we are absent one from another.'

I remembered the long yellow scarf that she had given me and bought another as if she were still alive and it was our first Christmas all over again.

I found the Montblanc 'Noblesse Oblige' pen her mother had given her and I thought it would be nice to use it to write about her. Perhaps it might help the words come, there could be consolation and reassurance as I wrote, with her voice at my shoulder rather than the usual demon of doubt.

But I couldn't quite work out if I needed a spare cartridge in the barrel and ended up jamming it in so that I couldn't close the pen properly or write with it at all. Looking up potential solutions on the internet, and employing my incompetent DIY (which had once seen a shelf collapse and me throwing a Hoover down the stairs when I couldn't find a way of opening the bag), I used a screw to try and pull it out and that got stuck too and so I had to send it to a pen repairer, and after I had done so, and while thinking about rewriting one of the Dr Johnson plays that we had done, I turned to his dictionary and looked up the definition of the word 'repair':

Repair: To restore after injury or dilapidation … to fill up anew, by putting something in place of what is lost.

I looked up other words:

Restore: To bring back, to retrieve.
Resuscitate: To stir up anew, to revive.
Resurrection: Revival from the dead; return from the grave. *He triumphs in his agonies whilst the soul springs*

forward to the great object which she has always had in view and leaves the body with an expectation of being remitted to her in a glorious and joyful resurrection. Spectator.

And I realised, on receiving the restored pen, that writing this with her nib was a way of her guiding me. The flow of ink and prose was a different kind of bloodstream, of both memory and inspiration. This was an act of recovery, where recollection, art and beauty could be the greatest consolation. These were small steps, word by word, sentence by sentence, page by page, in the new grammar of righting oneself, regaining balance, moving towards a way of making sense of all that had happened without entirely thinking about it. The unselfconscious flow was its own form of mindless tidying.

Dressing and Undressing

But what to do with the clothes that were left behind, in the wardrobe, by the bed and under the stairs, in the spare room and in St Monans: the frocks, the shoes, the jewellery, the outfits for special dinners and celebrations and … her wedding gown?

At our service of blessing in Lambeth Palace Chapel, Marilyn wore a full-length cotton needlecord dress in pillar-box red from the theatrical costumier Droopy and Browns. My father's press officer was appalled.

'The scarlet woman. What will the papers say?'

'They're not here,' he replied, thinking the whole thing rather amusing.

'Someone will tell them,' she said. 'No one's going to keep this quiet.'

But they did.

Marilyn liked to dress well and theatrically. Her wardrobe was full of spectacular garments that she never saved for 'best'. She wore them every day: an antique Japanese kimono that she 'borrowed' from the back of a costume store at a provincial theatre; a deep purple long-sleeved Issy Miyake blouse; a crew-neck Ralston dress in black and Prince of Wales check with a full-length curtain-ring zip; a cream cotton summer dress with a Japanese sunray pattern in red, black and sand; a black Lagenlook jacket with a fabulous wide collar that fastens with two large shiny buttons.

She loved vintage and was proud that she still had the Biba jacket she had bought in the late sixties. She was specific about colour, avoiding yellow and green, insisting they made her skin look gaunt, and generally wore clothes as boldly as those old Soviet posters in red, black and white, with accents of silver, pink and blue. We were amused when we went to an exhibition at the Ingleby Gallery only to find that Marilyn's dress was in the same blocks of colour as a Callum Innes painting. 'You must let me take a photograph of you in front of that,' I said. 'It's the perfect match. Woman as work of art.'

'Trying my best,' she said. 'You can send it to the girls.'

When she finished dressing and thought she was ready to go out she would turn to me and ask the same question her mother had always asked her father: 'Will I do?'

And I would say, of course, yes, you look marvellous, splendid, but we were never actually 'ready'. There was still the business of perfume and lipstick and finding the right handkerchief and checking her handbag. We were a good fifteen minutes away from leaving the house and all of this was before the whole business of considering the weather and deciding on the right kind of coat.

There was a duster in splattered black and silver; a high-collared ruched coat with contrasting horizontal stripes in black and burnt sienna; a white wool and polyester Moyuru coat-dress with a photocopied winter woodland design; a black and white Yiannis Karitsiotis woollen coat with two bright red front buttons; and a 'when I am old I shall wear purple' coat, a full-length lilac hooded foldaway mac in nylon and polyester.

She wore this to a memorial service in Southwark Cathedral. We were just about the last to arrive and were shown to our seats by a worried-looking steward in a tweed jacket and a battered straw bowler decorated with fake flowers. She had little pebble-rimmed glasses and looked like the kind of woman who would get bumped off in the first act of *Midsomer Murders*. Then I realised.

'My God, it's Alice.' (This was the woman before Marilyn that I nearly married.)

'Hello, James.'

'Darling, this is Alice.'

Marilyn looked at her and smiled. 'Well, I'm very pleased to meet you, Alice.'

The organ started up for the processional hymn and my 'near miss' made her way back to her seat. Just before the first words were sung, Marilyn turned to me and said, as brightly as possible, 'Any regrets?'

Sometimes, like the actress Beryl Reid, Marilyn started her outfit with the shoes. Even though Marilyn Monroe almost certainly did not say the words, she liked the quotation: 'Give a girl the right shoes and she can conquer the world.'

There were red suede ankle boots and pink leopard-skin court shoes and black etched-leather lace-ups. On our visits to London, she would buy reflective grey cycle sneakers, or neon-orange patent-leather derbies, or Gatsby black-and-gold peep-toes. They were flashes of style but also conversational starter-points. She thought it was good to give people something to talk about and, after she died, the women from the cleaning company we employed to keep the house going told me that they used to have a game of 'Guess which shoes Marilyn will be wearing today?'

There were twelve of these women, who cleaned from a rota in pairs. On the day of the funeral, they held a two-minute silence for her, wherever they were working. They all stopped whatever they were doing to remember her. I can't really write these words without crying.

Marilyn could never pass a jewellery stall in a holiday market, often looking for the gaudiest and kitschiest items they had: glass that caught the light, bright earrings in geometric shapes, clacking necklaces and statement brooches. One of her signature pieces of costume jewellery was a series of liquid-glass rings in the shape of a cube with different-coloured inks inside. People always asked where she got them (they are available online and cost £17) but she told them not to worry, she would send them one; and she did.

Her dress sense meant that she was always noticed, which meant that she was frequently robbed. On a long weekend in Prague someone tried to steal from her handbag every single day that we were there. When I suggested that perhaps, possibly, she might want to dress down a bit she said: 'What do you want me to do? Wear a fleece?'

One Christmas I gave her a red leather double-zipped handbag. Both girls agreed that it just said: 'Rob me now.'

After our friend Bridget from the BBC had all *her* jewellery stolen, she sat down and drew each item from memory for the purposes of police and insurance. Marilyn was so taken with the idea of drawing her own jewellery that she started to do the same, often noting when and where she had bought a piece:

A pair of vintage 1950s clasp earrings. Two perfectly shaped star fish. Three pearls set in each leaf – gold stud balls texturing the skin of the fish. I wore them on holidays to Crete and Skye. Bought London. £55 in 2002.

A pair of pearl and mother-of-pearl cascade earrings bought in Ischia.

A shell bracelet from Kate, 2001. A Christmas gift.

Turquoise blue glass earrings from Ischia.

Cream soapstone earrings strung on small wooden beads. Bought in Mallorca.

A giant shell pendant from Girona, Spain, iridescent opalesque strung on small wooden beads. Charlotte wore it in a school play.

The amber James brought back from Poland.

In the summer she always carried a Japanese paper fan in her handbag. Because she was so pale, she disliked the heat (which makes us wonder all the more about vitamin D deficiency as a possible cause of MND and its higher levels in Scotland). She enjoyed the dramatic flick of a fan, and knew how to rock the look, using it as a gestural punctuation point when closed, waving it like a Restoration actress when open, and even holding it just below her eyes as if she was Scotland's first geisha.

We once went to a High Table dinner at an Oxford college. She sat between two dons who didn't ask her a single question for the whole night. This is quite common in such situations, but Marilyn wasn't used to it. At first, she was delighted that the woman next to her was an expert in late-eighteenth-century fans, but then realised that her fellow-guest could talk about nothing else. On the way home, she was furious.

'I tried my best, darling, my absolute best, but it was USELESS. I asked her about seventeenth-century fans and nineteenth-century fans, but she said, no, she only knew about the eighteenth-century fans. I wanted to know about her favourite fans. She didn't have any. I asked her if she had any fans at home, if she collected fans herself, and she said she did not. I wondered if she had ever been asked to advise actors on how to hold a fan, but she said no, she hadn't. I asked her every possible question I could think of until I ran out. There was a silence and, *even then*, she didn't think to ask: "And what do you do?" Not even "Do you have a fan yourself?" I gave her two hours of opportunity to talk about her bloody fans. What are these people like? And by the way, she had absolutely no sense of style, no sense of humour and no imagination. She couldn't have been more dull, *even on the subject of fans, which should be fascinating*. We're never going to one of those bloody things again. Next time, you can go on your own. Unbelievable. Unforgivable. Really. Ridiculous.'

Even at the end of her disease and her life, there was a refusal to dress down. She wore a twisted turquoise-and-coral rope necklace with a magnetic clasp that was easy to put on and take off; Salvador Dalí earrings with a lobster and a telephone; and the room was filled with the scent of English Oak and Hazelnut.

Rosie helped her to decide what to wear from a selection of five or six outfits that were easy to manage and made her comfortable. I was seldom involved in this after Marilyn had a food spill at lunch and insisted that I change her dress. I made a bit of a hash of it with the sleeves and the back and the pulling it down and the checking that it was straight across the shoulders. When I had quite finished, she said, 'You've always been hopeless at putting on and taking off women's clothes. I blame myself. But I'm not going to start teaching you now.'

I remembered walking into a hotel restaurant on the day of our arrival for a short holiday in France. We were straight off the plane and the last to arrive and the dining room was full of the restrained chic of silent and judgemental Saturday diners on their day off. It was the kind of place where if you do talk then your only conversation is about the food and the white wine is stored in an ice bucket half a kilometre away to prevent you pouring it yourself.

Marilyn was wearing a peach-coloured floaty linen top. She had her neon-orange patent-leather derbies on her feet. Our fellow-guests gave her the twice-over. We ate and chatted away but the sophisticated locals kept on looking across as if warning us that, if we enjoyed ourselves too much, we wouldn't be able to appreciate the food.

We had the first asparagus of the season, lemon sole with French beans and a lavender crème brûlée. Although we had been the last to arrive, we appeared to be the first to finish. Marilyn pushed back her chair and stood up to leave. She smiled, put her hand to her lips and walked towards the door. Then she turned, made sure that all the sombre diners were looking at her and said to me very sternly: 'Now we go fucky fuck.'

She always had a great sense of timing. After she died, Susannah, a theatre critic, wrote to me saying that she wished she had known Marilyn better. 'Almost weekly on the radio I am caught up in a play, wait to hear the producer's name and find yet again it is Marilyn. She must constantly have made people listen differently and respond better: what a gift. Her style, too, comes back to me. I remember at a Bloomsbury party a few years ago, she was in blue-and-white swirls with a big collar. Alexandra

[Editor-in-Chief] commented on how washed-out some of the young were, and said: "Look at Marilyn – that's how it's done."'

One of her last productions was *A Portrait of a Gentleman* by Peter Ansorge. It was inspired by an account of Henry James clearing out the Venetian lodgings of his 'intimate friend' the 53-year-old novelist Constance Fenimore Woolson, who had committed suicide by throwing herself out of a second-storey window on 24 January 1894. In April, James opened the closed-up Casa Semitecolo with his friend's sister and was given responsibility for the author's literary remains. In them, he found sketches and ideas for novels, one of which was to inspire his short story 'The Beast in the Jungle'.

The story is about a man called John Marcher who is convinced that he has been marked out for something rich and strange, and that he will know the moment because it will be when the metaphorical 'beast in the jungle' pounces. But he fails to realise that his defining moment is not literary achievement but the love that is standing right in front of him: May Bartram. This character is modelled on Constance, a woman who was now dead and lost to him. James had missed his defining moment, caught up by distracted vanity, and was now faced with nothing but his own arid end for 'no passion had ever touched him'. Only after her death did he realise what he had missed.

According to his biographer Lyndall Gordon, as they finished clearing out the lodgings, James hired a gondolier to take Constance's dresses and throw them into the lagoon. 'But the dresses refused to drown. One by one they rose to the surface, their busts and sleeves swelling like black balloons. Purposefully, the gentleman pushed them under, but silent, irreproachful, they rose before his eyes.'

Marilyn was always taken with this idea: of the Venetian lagoon which we had often discussed as the place where we would like our ashes to be scattered, and of the stylish ballgowns in silk and taffeta that refuse to sink, even at the end of a gondolier's pole.

Style cannot be sunk.

Looking at her full wardrobe, I decided I was going to keep some of her clothes. The girls could have a rummage, but I would not separate them out or sell them or even take them to the Venetian lagoon and sink them myself. So, I have decided to leave them alone. I can even imagine the clothes talking to each other, with their own memories, telling of their adventures and their last outings and what it was like to be picked out and worn by Marilyn.

I went back to my desk and found a letter written to me by our friend Tom: 'Sitting here in the barn I can almost reach out and touch Marilyn across the table, no doubt with large bright buttons, red shoes, lots of rustling black silk. Marrying her was the best thing you ever did, wasn't it?'

It was.

The Kite

Marilyn hated having her photograph taken. She wanted it over and done with as quickly as possible even when I explained that the more trouble I took, the better the final image would be. She never trusted the camera, preferring to draw, and was useless at taking photographs herself. It just didn't interest her. Sometimes I thought she was deliberately bad at it, just as some men are hopeless with household tasks so they don't have to do them. The first photograph I ever took of her, outside her back door in Edinburgh, in red coat and black-and-white cotton gingham dress, carries a patient but suspicious look as if she is saying: 'Do you have to carry on with this? What are you going to do with it? I'm not at my best.'

At her best was always how she wanted to be.

She did allow photographs at our wedding. I took a picture of her turning round and smiling from a bench in Venice on our honeymoon that came to be used in her obituaries. I wanted people to use an image from when she was happy rather than sick. She was picky about who she allowed to take the photographs and was best when she was photographed unobserved. She hated being arranged into a photo-opportunity (someone else directing) or being asked to stare into bright sunlight on holiday with other people who didn't know how to take a decent picture. I had to keep explaining why she didn't like it and sometimes even ask people not to insist on photographing her as she really did absolutely hate it.

The more I worked in film and television, the more I began to understand lighting. Then I was given a bit more latitude and permission to sneak the odd photograph of Marilyn, especially when I told her the lessons I had learned from cameramen: how it was far better to shoot into the sun (the exact opposite to the childhood use of the Instamatic on summer holidays) and then use reflectors to provide most of the key and fill light; how Philip Bonham-Carter, who shot Delia Smith and the Queen, preferred to keep the cheek on a woman's face nearest the camera darker, so there was foreground shadow and the viewer would look into the frame and into the light; how the great Remi Adefarasin (*Truly, Madly, Deeply*; *About a Boy*; *Elizabeth*) employed a single light source behind Susan Wooldridge reading in bed in my film *Miss Pym's Day Out*, using the open book to bounce the light back into her face like Rembrandt's *An Old Woman Reading*.

Marilyn was amused by my account of filming the most famous woman I had ever met, the legendary Lauren Bacall, who didn't charge a fee but insisted on a suite at the Algonquin in New York together with her own driver, make-up and hairstylist, as well as approval of the lighting, the camera angle and a longer-than-usual portrait lens. No wide-angle nonsense, no shooting from below the eyeline, no direct light, and everything bounced apart from a soft 'butterfly light' for the eyes, as used by Josef von Sternberg for Marlene Dietrich. The cameraman was my friend Jeremy Pollard and it took two and a half hours to get right. When Marilyn saw the final film (it was a documentary about Henry Moore) she said, 'Well, that's it, then. You just have to photograph me like I'm Lauren Bacall.'

And from then on, we had no overhead lights in the house, just reading lamps, wall-lights and candles. Everything had to be softly beautiful. We had to live, even though we were in a terraced house at the end of a cul-de-sac in St Albans at the time, as if we only existed in a Vermeer painting with a Chardin still life on the kitchen table and a Rembrandt on the wall.

Fortunately, Charlotte has become a very good photographer and so when we decided to renew our vows for our twenty-fifth wedding anniversary, she offered to take all the pictures as her present to us. It was an incredibly moving occasion, a mixture of thankfulness, celebration and showing off. 'We might as well do this properly,' said Marilyn, 'we're not going to have another chance.' Pip Torrens read the Shakespeare sonnet 'When forty winters shall besiege thy brow', Siobhán Redmond had learned 'My love is like a red, red rose' and Bill Paterson read the Gospel account of the wedding at Cana in the Scots translation by William Lorimer. He performed it as if he had just come from the scene and was telling the story as an anecdote to his friends in the pub.

'TWA DAYS EFTERHIN there wis a waddin at Cana in Galilee. Jesus's mither was there, an Jesus an his disciples wis amang the friends bidden til it. Efter a while the wine was aa dune, an his mither said til him, "They hae nae mair wine."

'"Ye can lae that tae me," said Jesus; "my hour isna come."'

Charlotte's photographs of the occasion are nearly all observational rather than posed and they focus on the details: the silver rings on our hands; Marilyn rehearsing the singers and listening attentively to her friends, unobserved and at her best. It is this sense of her being involved in life that shines out most strongly. Perhaps her distrust of photography came from the fact she had to stop for it. It was posed. It didn't feel real. It took time out of the business of living, of getting things done. 'He who binds himself to a joy,' I can hear her beginning and me interrupting and finishing the Blake quotation, 'DOES THE WINGÈD LIFE DESTROY. Just as long as you don't mind being "binded" to me.'

'Always binded. You know that. Too late to get out of it now.'

When she was ill, I had to take her photograph for her Blue Badge, not that we were going out much. 'Don't show me,' she said, 'I can't bear to see it,' and her look in the photograph was the first time I ever saw her defeated by illness. It says, 'I told you I hated having my photograph taken. I know you have to, but I still hate it and now it has come to this and there is nothing either of us can do about it.'

But this wasn't the last image. There is one of her in St Monans in a red bobble hat on that last Midsummer Day, of her smiling back at me, tender and full of thirty-five years of love, patience, tenderness and acknowledgement. There is also a final blurred and accidental image of the inside of her hand, with its last strange baby-like softness, taken by accident on my phone.

Then, just before she died, her friend Eileen sent us a black-and-white photograph. It is of Marilyn flying a kite on the beach, looking up, full of delight and glee and joy.

She is excited and happy and it became one of the images we chose to send out and remember her by. It is at the front of this book.

Two weeks later, Gerda Stevenson gave us this poem.

Old Photograph of a Young Woman

(in memoriam Marilyn Imrie, 1947–2020)

I didn't know you then,
wind-blown lass, happed
in your winter coat –
time was all ahead,
like the kite you guide
on a single gossamer thread
and only you can see,
its flight path beyond the frame;

everything is light
in this faded black and white –
your skin, your smile, the sky,
the bright sand of a Fife shore,
your future flying before.

White Tulips

On Valentine's Day 1985, the year in which we married, I gave Marilyn a bunch of forty white tulips. I didn't want to do the cliché of twelve red roses, or twenty-five, or fifty of anything. I wanted something simple and different and wrapped in brown paper. I never realised this would become a tradition, but I soon came to know that if I ever failed to do this over the next thirty-five years it would be an unforgivable black mark. She told me of a line from a sequence of poems, dedicated to her, that she had directed before we met, by another Marilyn, the Canadian writer Marilyn Bowering, about the most famous Marilyn of all time, Marilyn Monroe. It was called 'Anyone Can See I Love You'.

> *If ever you can walk into a room*
> *And not come first to me:*
> *whatever your reasons are,*
> *they are not enough.*

This became the number-one rule of our marriage and white tulips became the floral signature of my devotion. We would stop whenever we saw them. I sought out references to them in art and literature: in Elizabeth Blackadder's watercolours, in the photographer John Blakemore's *The Stilled Gaze*, where they lie post-coitally on a table, in Deborah Moggach's novel *Tulip Fever* and in Sylvia Plath's poem featuring tulips that open 'like the mouth of some great African cat'.

Marilyn loved the way tulips stood proud in a glass vase and then fell away, relaxed and unashamed in the coming days. I found myself giving her other presents that were also simple, minimalist and white, perhaps because they provided a sense of cleanliness, erasure and starting again. Looking back over these memories, I found another reference to the colour in a message I had placed in *The Times* on our very first Valentine's Day, full of adolescent admiration: 'Oh white giraffe, see how the happy thrush loves you!'

I should have been chucked on the spot. What on earth was this nonsense? It's only one step away from couples who speak baby-talk. But I remembered how Marilyn had told me how peaceful and elegant she thought white giraffes were, identifying with their oddity and difference. That's why I must have referred to her in the same way, as something magical, rare and beautiful, as mythical as a unicorn, but real, and here on earth.

And this is how our relationship seems now, as something out of dream and myth, as ghostly as the sight of white giraffes standing and staring back at the camera before walking elegantly away. I can't quite believe either that it happened at all or that it is over: or, at least, 'over' in the physical, earthly sense.

I can't look at white tulips without thinking of her and wanting to take them to the grave. I discovered there was a tulip called *Tulipa* 'Marilyn' and even though it wasn't one she would have particularly liked, in red and white (she preferred single colours), I ordered a hundred and planted them as soon as they arrived because I was impatient.

I thought of us coming over from Edinburgh, at the height of the first lockdown when it wasn't allowed but the doctor told us, 'For God's sake just go,' so that she could see the tulips in our garden in St Monans for the last time, and I remembered, when we finally had to leave, wheeling her away in the wheelchair she hated and her crying out the line from Walter de la Mare's poem 'Fare Well': 'Look thy last on all things lovely …'

I wondered if I would ever get used to the sadness of this loss. When I first wanted to be a writer, I copied out a passage from *Next Time I'll Sing to You*, a play by James Saunders, in which a character talks about the way in which grief is a kind of universal undercurrent beneath all our behaviour, and I reread my O level copy of Wordsworth's 'Tintern Abbey' in which I had underlined the passage about 'the still sad music of humanity' as if I had known what this was like and what it meant. I was seventeen at the time and didn't have a clue.

At the end of our friend Shelagh Stephenson's play, *The Memory of Water*, written shortly after the death of her mother, the character of Mary leaves the family home for a funeral in the freezing winter snow and is asked about her future: 'What are you going to do?'

And she replies: 'Learn to love the cold.'

So this is what I found myself doing, living with the memory of my wife in the middle of a pandemic Scottish winter, picking up tips on how to live on my own for the first time in my life. I was advised to do nothing irreversible in the first year of mourning; to make sure I took exercise;

197

to phone a friend every day and be kind to myself. Rosie reminded me: 'You have no skin.'

I was told to eat properly and follow a routine and not drink too much alcohol, preferably none at all. Batch cooking helped, apparently. Then I could just 'take things out of the freezer' and I wouldn't have to 'waste time' cooking again and again. But I quite wanted to waste that time, and watch football, and read and write and talk to friends. I had plenty of time to waste, and then later, after I had thought about this, a song came on the radio, a hit from the eighties, Owen Paul singing 'You're My Favourite Waste of Time'. I told Rosie that I thought I had given it to one of my old girlfriends.

'You did,' she replied. 'You gave it to my mother. On vinyl.'

Julie sent me exotic Ottolenghi recipes that might as well begin: 'First fly to Tel Aviv.' I watched cookery programmes on television, but I was brought short when I saw Nigella Lawson wearing the same Venetian dressing gown that Charlotte had given Marilyn two Christmases ago: a cream and pale blue map of the city in the lightest silk. It was surreal to see Nigella wearing it. I watched her creating a dish that called for Aleppo pepper, and it seemed so incongruous to be making something with pepper from Syria that I phoned Pip and ranted at him and he said, 'I know, what next? White Helmet risotto?'

I read other people's memoirs for comfort: Joan Didion's *The Year of Magical Thinking*, Alison Light's *A Radical Romance*, C. S. Lewis's *A Grief Observed*, Gillian Rose's *Love's Work*, Ian Ridley's *The Breath of Sadness*; all those harrowing accounts of widows and widowers so stunned by loss that their only way back was to try and write their way out of it.

It's inevitable for any writer to want to do this because there can be no other subject. How can you concentrate on making up stuff for some stupid novel when you've just lost the love of your life?

Despite the company, I questioned why I, too, was writing a memoir and if this book was really for anyone other than me? What could I add, not so much to the gaiety of nations but to the community of sorrow?

But then I thought that this book was about *Marilyn*. That would make it different, because there was no one like her and never would be and she was going to see me through all this. It was almost as if we were writing it together, as had been the case with all my writing in the past. But this had to be true and like us and so, as well as being sad and serious, it had to be larky and daffy and full of life: a reversal of 'in the midst of life we are in death', becoming instead 'in the midst of death we are in life'. Reading it, I thought, should be like meeting her for the first time, or her walking into a room, smiling and perfumed and fabulously dressed and people thinking: Thank God, she's here. I don't have to worry. I can relax now.

It used to annoy me whenever I went to parties on my own. People would immediately say, 'Where's Marilyn?' as if my presence alone was not good enough. But now I realise it was because they could not imagine me without her.

Well, they can now.

I read in the *New York Times* of a couple who had only just met when the pandemic began, and how they had to sustain their love when they were apart. One of them told the reporter: 'I think the reason we have lasted was because we always tried to be thankful for having met, instead of questioning that we were separated.'

Gratitude is part of love. I remembered my father's bold assertion in the Bible he gave us that 'Love never fails' with its confident underlining. I looked up the promises of Christ in St Paul's Letter to the Romans: *For I am persuaded, that neither death, nor life, nor angels, nor principalities, nor powers, nor things present, nor things to come, nor height, nor depth, nor any other creature, shall be able to separate us from the love of God, which is in Christ Jesus our Lord.*

Sometimes this is hard to hold on to. There's a grave near Marilyn's in St Monans which has the inscription: 'If love could have saved you, you would have lived forever.'

Most of the tombstones talk of eternal rest and are appropriate for a fishing village: 'Life's storms are passed for evermore' and 'After storms safe harbour'. There is Protestant modesty too: 'Worthy of remembrance' as if some people are NOT worthy. Other inscriptions are uncompromisingly straightforward: 'No time left'. Several compare the transience of life with the promises of Jesus: 'With Christ – which is better'.

Rosie joked that they should have added a question mark and then we had a blasphemous laugh and I asked: 'Which is better? Christ? Or Marilyn?'

'That's a tough one …'

'I think I'd rather have Marilyn.'

We shared this grave humour and I was struck by how cheerful some of the other inscriptions were and how they quoted from the favourite phrases of their beloved dead. 'Man up!' Another had the invocation: 'Smile, smile, smile'.

Joint graves talked of couples being 'reunited' and 'together at last'. But I did not think it needed my death to join me with my wife because I did not feel separated from her at all. Broken but not separated.

I held on to a perfect palm-fit pebble that I asked Lida to carve for me before she did the gravestone, with the 'M' on one side, the 'J' on the other, a portable memento. It was and is like carrying a piece of the grave.

Sometimes, I take it out and pass it from hand to hand. I put it on the table by my side when I am writing. It says: 'Marilyn is here.'

When I wrote to people to thank them for their condolences, I had a card designed to make it easier and special. It was based on the definitions of the word 'Marilyn' as 'wished-for child', 'beloved' and 'star of the sea'. It read:

In the darkest of skies
A sea of starlight

Despite the convenience of the card, I still took trouble over what I wrote inside – after all, what else was I going to do to fill the time and what could be more important than this?

I said that all recognition was a gift of grace, and that grief was unpredictable. We know people can't live forever but, as with all that is awful, we hope to be spared, or at least for the inevitable to be delayed. And now there is the loss, but also the grace and privilege of knowing Marilyn, a woman as rare as a white giraffe, and for a love to be known and experienced and remembered and lived with and comforted by. Perhaps the boundaries between life and death are more permeable than we think.

On the first Valentine's Day without her, I laid white tulips on the graveyard grass, on the spot where I knew her heart should be. I looked down and I didn't know what to think or say; but I did recall the end of Henry James's story 'The Beast in the Jungle', when Marcher visits the tomb of his dead love: 'What it all amounted to, oddly enough, was that in his finally so simplified world this garden of death gave him the few square feet of earth on which he could still most live.'

I wondered what it might be like to throw myself down on to the ground, just as Marcher does. I could lie down on Marilyn's grave, on *our* grave, and wait for the wind and the rain and the darkness. It would certainly make it easier for the undertaker, who could simply move me to one side, summon the gravedigger and tip me in.

Hypothermia. It would be one way to go.

I remembered Siobhán telling me her plan, when the time came and she thought she had really had enough of life, to drink a bottle of vodka and crawl under 'the hedge of doom'; and of my friend Sarah telling me that when she nearly died of hypothermia, while swimming in the sea, 'it was rather lovely'.

But this is an indulgence and a fantasy. I must keep on living with grief and possibility and the hope of adventure. Friends tell me: 'It's what she'd want you to do.'

But is it? Really? Marilyn didn't seem that keen on my future life without her. She did her best but I think – no, I know – she *hated* the idea of her life without me and my life without her. She was furious about not being able to spend more time as a grandmother (she had less than three years), or as a mother, or as a friend and even as a wife. She was unspeakably depressed, *literally unspeakably*, by the inevitability of death. There was nothing I could do, *absolutely nothing*, to make her accept it, or ready herself for it. The greatest tragedy was to see someone so optimistic, so cheerful and such a force for good in the world, a woman who could change the mood of a room just by walking into it and saying, 'Hello Gorgeousness', brought low and into such despair.

What I do know is that my task now is to live for her, to try to continue a love that is both real and imaginary; to incorporate her velocity of character and all that was best in her, celebrating the fact that we knew and loved each other for as long as we did.

This is my duty, I think, as I lay the white tulips on her grave. It is my calling, my task, and my great good fortune, to have been given the grace of such a love.

Not the End

Honeymoon, Venice, November 1985

Acknowledgements

Thank you to Gerda Stevenson for her poem 'The Kite', to Marilyn Bowering for 'Anyone Can See I Love You', to Shelagh Stephenson for allowing a quotation from *The Memory of Water*, and to the Ingleby Gallery and Andrew Cranston for use of their exhibition catalogue *But the Dream Had No Sound*. Sorley MacLean's poem 'Shores' from *Poems to Eimhir* is reprinted by kind permission of Carcanet Press, Manchester, UK and the poet's daughter, Ishbel MacLean.

Thank you to Hildegard Bechtler, Georgina Brown, Susannah Clapp, Michelle Green, Marcia Haig, Anna Keay, Stuart Rock, Crispin Simon and Tom Stuart-Smith for permission to cite their letters. Thank you to John Butt, Louise Dobbin, Deborah Findlay, Rachel Foster, Rachel Fox, Neil Gardner, Beth Holgate, Florence and Richard Ingleby, Bridget Kendall, Lida Kindersley, Anna Ledgard, Allan Little, Liz Lochhead, Joanna MacGregor, Juliette Mead, Teresa Monachino, Marion Nancarrow, Bill Paterson, Sarah Power, Jane Raven, Siobhán Redmond, Heather Smith, Alan Stephen, Pip Torrens, Harriet Walter, Jo Willett and Richard Williams for stories included here and for their sustaining friendship.

Thank you to everyone at MND Scotland and Eidyn Care and to all the district nurses at NHS Scotland. Thank you to Dr Ali Joy, Dr Anne-Louise Jennings, Dr Sue Stuart-Smith, Dr Graham Russell, Dr Jane Wilson and St Columba's Hospice.

Thank you to Marilyn's fellow producers: Catherine Bailey, Eoin O'Callaghan and Gordon Kennedy.

Thank you to everyone at Bloomsbury: my adored editor Alexandra Pringle, Allegra Le Fanu, Sarah-Jane Forder and Philippa Cotton.

Thank you to my agent David Godwin for unswerving loyalty, steadfast wisdom and unerring immediacy.

Thank you to all my friends, both mentioned and not mentioned.

Thank you to my beloved sister Rebecca and her family, and to Rosie and Charlotte, Sean and Bea for everything. And welcome, Anwen, whom Marilyn would have adored.

Thank you to you, the reader, for reading this. Seize the day, remember well, love fiercely.

A Note on the Type

The text of this book is set in Bembo, which was first used in 1495 by the Venetian printer Aldus Manutius for Cardinal Bembo's *De Aetna*. The original types were cut for Manutius by Francesco Griffo. Bembo was one of the types used by Claude Garamond (1480–1561) as a model for his Romain de l'Université, and so it was a forerunner of what became the standard European type for the following two centuries. Its modern form follows the original types and was designed for Monotype in 1929.